WHICH NAME FITS?

An animal with real style and charm	Pizzazz
A cat who sleeps all day	PJ
Your pet's a winner!	Ribbons
You're an artist	Renoir
Your pet is an adorable bulldog	Roseanne
A dog who won't stay home	Rover
A pet with big eyes	Saucer
A willful pet	Scarlett
A good listener	Therapy
A courageous cat	Thurgood
Just a great name for any animal	Theodore

... and there's plenty more!

5,001 NAMES FOR YOUR PET

RITA BLOCKTON

AVON BOOKS ■ NEW YORK

5,001 NAMES FOR YOUR PET is an original publication of Avon
Books. This work has never before appeared in book form.

AVON BOOKS
A division of
The Hearst Corporation
1350 Avenue of the Americas
New York, New York 10019

Copyright © 1995 by Rita Blockton
Published by arrangement with the author
Library of Congress Catalog Card Number: 95-94306
ISBN: 0-380-78040-2

First Avon Books Printing: November 1995

AVON TRADEMARK REG. U.S. PAT. OFF. AND IN OTHER COUNTRIES, MARCA REGIS-
TRADA, HECHO EN U.S.A.

Printed in the U.S.A.

RA 10 9 8 7 6 5 4 3 2 1

Preface

Congratulations!
    Presumably you're about to buy, or have just gotten, a dog, cat, gerbil, cockatoo—just had a litter of something—or maybe you're taking over a farm and have hundreds of wonderful cows or horses to name! Whatever it might be, if you're anything like me, half the fun of getting a new animal is naming it.

At first I tried to stay away from the usual—Tuffy, Taffy, Ginger (you wouldn't believe how many Gingers there are), Rover and Fido (you wouldn't believe how few Rovers and Fidos there are). Well, in the end, I included them all. Hours in the library, at the vet's, looking through baby name books, magazines, television shows, dictionaries, thesauruses, almanacs, looking around rooms, calling my friends . . . generally obsessing, as I tend to do.

Of course, I must admit that I made up a lot of them myself. Naming things is something I love to do. It all started in high school when I made up the name for our winter dance.

I actually won the naming contest! The Snow Ball (what can I tell you?). So, while not exactly brilliant, I won two tickets to the dance and, if you can imagine, that started me on a lifetime of naming things. (Now why couldn't I have won something everyone would have remembered me for, like a beauty contest?! No one ever forgets who wins that. I can assure you that no one even remembers that fateful dance, no less the name! No less who named it!)

But, since this seems to be my "thing," I hope you can sit back and enjoy looking through this book . . . and, with any luck, find the purrfect name for your pet!

Rita Blockton

A & D	For a pet that helps with the baby diapers
A & E	For an arts and entertainment type
A & P	For a pet you take grocery shopping
A & R	A pet for someone in the record industry
A. M.	For a morning pet
ABACUS	A mathematician's pet
ABBEY CAT	Perfect for an Abyssinian
ABBOTT	For someone whose first name is Bud or last name is Costello
ABC	*See* "Triples" for his brothers NBC and CBS
ABDUL-JABBAR	A basketball fan's pet
ABDULLAH	A pharaoh hound or sloughi ... originally from Egypt
ABE	My father's name ... nice, kind, good cook ... a saluki, elegant, affectionate, friendly with children, a perfect match
ABEL	Pair with Cain

ABERCROMBIE	The great clothing store Abercrombie & Fitch ... 57th Street in Manhattan ... malls here and there
ABIGAIL	For a blue-cream point Himalayan, very female
ABIGAYLE	From Hebrew: Father is rejoicing. You notice that's not my name.
ABNER	*Lil Abner* ... the cartoon series
ABOU	Means "father" in Arabic. So probably a good name for a stud animal.
ABRACADABRA	A wonderful name for a pet that keeps disappearing
ABRAHAM	The formal version of my father's name, Abe. Still nice, kind, and a good cook ... even more appropriate for a saluki
ABSOLUT	Good for a Swedish elkhound
ABSTRACT	For a pet with strange markings
ACE	The ace of hearts. Although, it seems like a real guy name.
ACHILLES	Heel!
ACTOR	For any animal that knows how to get the better of you
ADELE	It's so sheeplike. Wouldn't this be a great name for a Bedlington terrier?
ADELSON	Good for a Pyrenees mastiff ... powerful, big, silent, friendly, and not too interested in food (what a concept)
ADIEU	A pet for someone who travels a lot
AD LIB	For any animal that can talk you into something
ADMIRAL	This is perfect for a bulldog that likes to bark orders
ADOLFO	It would have to be a very well-dressed pet

ADOLPH	A good meat tenderizer . . . a German shepherd or a Doberman pinscher
ADONIS	A great-looking male. No one I know. No one I'll ever meet. Perfect for your best of breed
ADRIAN	YO!!!
AEROSMITH	Great rock stars and performers
AERSOSTAR	Great for any type of bird
AESOP	When your pet is a fable
AFRICA	As in *Out Of* . . . Meryl Streep and Robert Redford
AFRICAN QUEEN	Perfect for a black Turkish Angora . . . lush coat and regal looking
AFRICAN VIOLET	A white Turkish Angora . . . lush coat, not as regal looking as the queen
AGAMEMNON	From Greek: myth, king of Mycenae during Trojan War . . . killed by his wife, Clytemnestra
AGASSI	A tennis fan's pet
AGATHA	A wonderful name for big females . . . Saint Bernards, Black and tan coonhounds, borzois
AGATHA CHRISTIE	The great criminal mind of Agatha Christie . . . great for a sneaky cat
AGENT 99	Pair with Maxwell Smart
AGGIE	Nickname of Agnes
AGNES	Sounds so downtrodden. But, so great for a cat
AGNEW	An American fox terrier . . . feisty and a scrapper
AHAB	Wicked king of Israel . . . husband of Jezebel . . . great name for a fish

AHMED	An Arabic name ... a sloughi is directly decended from royal Egyptian dogs ... docile, obedient, and affectionate
AÏDA	An opera lover's pet
AIRBAG	A car salesman's pet
AIRBORNE	A pilot or stewardess' pet
AJAX	A cleaning fanatic's pet
AKBAR	For an Afghan hound, ancient breed ... courageous, sweet, and intelligent
AKIKO	A Japanese bobtail or Japanese spitz
AKIMBO	Means, basically, bowlegged ... it has to be an English bulldog or any animal that waddles rather than walks
ALABAMA	Would have to be a sexy southern belle
À LA CARTE	A waiter's pet
ALADDIN	It came with a lamp
À LA MODE	An ice cream fanatic's pet
ALBA	Albacore's nickname
ALBACORE	Tuna ... great name for a fish or cat
ALBEE	Perfect for a Woolf ... a Virginia Woolf
ALBERT	Royalty ... for a truly regal animal For a prince of a pet
ALBERTA	Royalty ... for a truly regal, female animal
ALBERTO	For a regal pet that uses hair products
ALCOTT	For a Louisa May fan
ALDEN	For a calico long-haired Scottish fold ... placid and adorable
ALDO	A pet that brings a "Ray" of sunshine into your life

ALEX	Good name for a Great Dane
ALEXANDER	For a more formal Great Dane
ALEXANDER THE GREAT	For an exceptional Great Dane
ALF	He wsa once the rage of TV
ALFALFA	Ran around with Buckwheat in "The Little Rascals"
ALFONSE	Perfect for a snooty dog
ALFONSO	A deposed king of Spain or a Spanish mastiff
ALFRED	Batman's butler, great for a superhero's sidekick
ALFREDO	A pasta lover's pet
ALGEBRA	A mathematician's pet
ALI	Usually for a cat ... nice for a Boxer terrier too
ALIAS	A criminal's pet
ALI BABA	The poor woodcutter in *The Arabian Nights*
ALIBI	A liar's pet
ALI CAT	For a stray
ALICE B. TOKLAS	For a pet that likes brownies
ALIEN	For a Devon rex, Cornish res, sphynx ... all hairless cats. Then you have the Chinese crested dog, also hairless.
ALIMONY	A disgruntled divorcee's pet
ALISTAIR	Must be a good cook
ALIWISHES	What ever Ali wants, Ali gets
ALKA-SELTZER	For a pet that drives you crazy either by barking too much or missing the litter box too much
ALLENDALE	A Florida pet

ALLERGY   Good for a shedding animal

ALMA   Another perfect animal name. Large or small, ugly or cute, it fits.

ALOHA   A Hawaiian traveler's pet

ALONZO   Great cat name! Perfect for the basketball fan

ALTHEA   Lovely for a pretty golden Persian, Himalayan, or anything fluffy

ALVA   Good for a nonfluffy pet ... short hair and muscular ... bulldogs, beagles, German shorthaired pointers

ALVIN   A chipmunk or a dancer's name

AMADEUS   For a very intense, preferably musically inclined pet

AMANDA   An American curl longhair

AMARETTO   A blue mitted ragdoll, or your typical alcoholic-reference pet, the Saint Bernard

AMARYLLIS   A soft-coated wheaten terrier, or any pet with a flowery personality ... triple with Peony and Daisy

AMAZON   BIG, BEAUTIFUL, and FEMALE

AMBASSADOR   Good name for a pet that likes to greet visitors at the door

AMBER   A red spotted tabby exotic shorthair. (Cats can certainly have very long names.)

AMBROSE   One of my favorites. Good for nearly any animal, but how about a harlequin Great Dane?

AMBROSIA   One of my favorite desserts

AMELIA   Good name for a bird. To follow in Amelia Earhart's footsteps

AMERICA   A patriot's pet

AMERCIAN EXPRESS	For a patriot who likes to charge
AMETHYST	For your gem
AMNESIA	A forgetful person's pet
AMOROUS	A gigolo's pet
AMOS	If your name is Andy
AMPLIFIER	Parrots, mynah birds, macaws, etcetera
AMSTEL	Good for a lite pet
AMTRAK	Good for a fast pet
AMY	A cute name for a cocker spaniel
ANALYST	A stockbroker or a psychiatrist's pet
ANASTASIA	It makes me think of "amnesia," which I will now add to the list
ANCHORS AWAY	Good for a fish, or a pet for a sailor
ANCHOVY	I would think that any cat would love this.
ANDORA	For a nice, big tortie and white Maine coon
ANDRÉ	For a French bulldog, or for a tennis fan
ANDY	What a name for a ragdoll! (That is a breed of cat . . . and one that I happen to own too.)
ANDY HARDY	For a sweet, open-faced, guileless pet
ANGEL	Well, at first aren't they all. You know best if it applies.
ANGELICA	Definitely for a pet from Houston
ANGELO	For an Italian pointer . . . elegant, thougtful, loyal, and not very cheerful
ANGUS	Okay. So, it's a great name for a bull. But think of an Irish setter or an Irish wolfhound.

ANITA	For an uphill pet
ANNE OF CLEVES	Pair with Henry VIII
ANNETTE	Great for a poodle, or someone who liked the Mouseketeers
ANNIE	A very nice, basic name for any orphaned animal
ANNIE GET YOUR GUN	For someone who lives with PMS, or for a hunter
ANNIE HALL	For a pet with long, straight hair, a bit confused, probably doesn't work, and is partial to sunglasses
ANNIE OAKLEY	For someone who likes riding western
ANN MARGRET	Beautiful redhead . . . golden retriever, Irish setter
ANN TAYLOR	For a pet that likes traditional dress, good shoes, and a good job
ANSEL	A photographer's pet
ANTIGONE	Oedipus' daughter
ANTOINE	A long-haired dachshund . . . I think it's a hysterical combination (but, I'm always my best audience)
ANTOINETTE	Marie's last name
ANTON	For a French bulldog
ANTONIO	A wirehaired dachshund . . . almost as hysterical as Antoine
ANTONY	A pet for a Marc, pair with Cleopatra
APACHE	A southwestern pet
APERTURE	A photographer's pet
APHRODITE	A Greek goddess . . . any pet you think is gorgeous

APOLLO	The Greek god of music, poetry, prophecy, and medicine. Wonderful for big, powerful animals.
APPLE BROWN BETTY	A brown classic tabby American shorthair
APPLEBY	A white classic tabby American longhair
APPLE PIE	A red classic tabby American shorthair
APPLESAUCE	A mixture
APRICOT	My favorite jam . . . and good for an orange colored pet
AQUARIUS	A January baby
AQUAVIT	A hundred proof baby
ARABELLA	An Egyptian mau or a cream point Himalayan
ARABESQUE	A pet with elaborately decorative markings
ARABIAN KING	For either a horse or a big, beautiful animal like a Russian wolfhound, Irish wolfhound, etcetera
ARAMIS	A pet that smells good
ARBERRY	Universal . . . cats, dogs, birds, gerbils
ARCHER	Someone good with a bow and arrow
ARCHIBALD	Great, strong name . . . perhaps for a bloodhound, Great Dane, or Great Pyrenees
ARCHIE	A pet for a Betty, Veronica, or Jughead
ARDEN	An animal with great skin
ARETHA	A great schnauzer would certainly get a ''little respect''
ARF	For a silent dog

ARGYLE	Definitely for a tortoise cat
ARI	Aristotle's nickname
ARIEL	A flier's pet
ARISTOCAT	A feline aristocrat
ARISTOCRAT	An Afghan ... regal and dignified
ARISTOPHANES	For a dramatic pet
ARISTOTLE	Ari's full name. A bulldog would be very good, as would a boxer.
ARIZONA	For someone into iced tea
ARLENE	Perfect for a beagle. Don't ask me why.
ARLINGTON	For a national minded pet
ARLO GUTHRIE	How about an American foxhound?
ARMAND	Very international, sophisticated name
ARMANI	An Italian pointer, into clothes, of course
ARMORY	A guard dog name
ARMSTRONG	For someone with strong arms, or a linoleum floor
ARMY ARCHERD	It would have to be a bald pet. Perhaps a French bulldog or a Devon rex or an archer's pet
ARNOLD	I can only think of Schwarzenegger when I see that name now. But it would be great for a basset hound.
ARPÈGE	A perfumed pet
ARPEL	A designer pet
ARQUIMEDES	A dalmatian
ARROW	A dachshund ... straight and narrow
ARSENIO	A pet for a night owl
ART DECO	For anyone partial to the forties

ARTHUR	Legendary king of England who led the Knights of the Round Table.
ARTURO	For an Italian greyhound . . . loves peaceful people but frightened of children
ARTURO TOSCANINI	A spinone Italiano. A very cute, wiry, big dog from France. But, the Italiano part went with the arturo
ARUBA	Good swimming name . . . a fish name perhaps
ASCOT	For someone who doesn't like to wear ties
ASH	For any gray colored animal
ASHLEY	Rhett and Scarlett were partial to him . . . in their own ways
ASHTON	For an Old English sheepdog or a puli
ASIA	Nice name for a Chinese Shar-pei (the wrinkled dog)
ASIMOV	For someone into science fiction
ASKHIM	When you want to know who made the poop in the living room . . . Askhim
ASPARAGUS	Any of your green varieties
ASPEN	A skier's pet
ASTA	The wirehaired terrier from "The Thin Man" series. Nick and Nora Charles
ASTAIRE	Pair with Rogers
ASTRO	The dog in "The Jetsons"
ATHENA	The goddess of wisdom, skills, and warfare. Any pet would be proud to have that as its name.

ATHENS   The capital of Greece, so a Greek hound, found only in Greece . . . lively and has a good sense of smell

ATLANTA   Capital of Georgia . . . a southern pet

ATLANTIS   Legendary island in the Atlantic west of Gibraltar, said to have sunk

ATLAS   BIG STRONG MALE

ATTILA   Good name for a Hun

AUDIT   The pet of an IRS agent or an accountant

AUGIE   This definitely sounds like a mixed breed

AUGUSTUS   For someone who likes the time of the Roman emperor Augustus, B.C. 27–14 A.D.

AULD LANG SYNE   For a pet you get for old times' sake

AUNTIE   A nurturing pet. A Newfoundland.

AUNTIE EM   I like this for bigger breeds, though it works for minis too

AUNTIE MAME   A pet that never stays put

AUNT JEMIMA   A nice, big, fat mamma! Newfoundland or Saint Bernard would be adorable

AURELIA   A Lakeland terrier . . . affectionate, spirited, and tenacious

AUREOLE   Fancy Manhattan restaurant. A bird name

AURORA   For a stargazer or a bore

AUSSIE   An Australian animal . . . Koalas

AUSTIN   Another Texas pet

AUTHOR   A writer's pet

AUTUMN   A pet that sheds

AVALON	A pet for a Frankie or an Annette
AVANTI	Someone who is always in a hurry
AVENGER	What a name for a guard dog! Like a rottweiler, German shepherd, pit bull, etcetera
AVERY	Murphy Brown's boy
AVIS	A pet for someone in the car rental business
AVON	A pet for someone in the skin product or publishing businesses
AXL	For a pet with tattoos, or, shall we say, markings
AXLE	For a pet that chases cars
AYATOLLAH	For a mean, dictatorial pet
AZALEA	A landscape architect's pet
AZTEC	A pet that comes to you from south of the border.
AZURE	A Skye terrier

B-12	The pet that really perks you up
B-2	For a bird or a bomber
BABBITT	The rabbit
BABE	For a blue ox, or a dog that likes baseball
BABETTE	A cook's pet ... someone who enjoys a feast
BABY	Another thing to "bring up"
BABY DEER	For a baby deerhound
BACALL	Bogie's baby
BACCARAT	For an absolutely crystal-clear pet
BACH	A musician's pet
BACKGAMMON	A pet for a game player
BACON	For a pet with high cholesterol
BADGES	For someone aspiring to law enforcement
BAGEL	Triple with Baguette and Bialy
BAGUETTE	A French poodle or perhaps a dachshund (long and narrow)
BAILEY	Double with Barnum ... a circus pet

BAKER	For a pet that can whip up a good meringue
BAKLAVA	For a sweet, little Greek pet
BALLERINA	Adorable for a bulldog
BALLY	For someone into shoes
BALLYHOO	For the adventurous pet
BALTHUS	Twentieth-century artist ... good name for a beefy kind of pet
BALZAC	Behind every great fortune there is a crime
BAMBI	For a deer pet
BAMM BAMM	For a ''Flintstones'' fan
BANANA BREAD	For a monkey or any primate without a movable thumb
BANDIT	A raccoon, any pet that steals your slippers, or Smokey's (the stock car driver from the movie) pal
BANKER	Perfect for a pet pig
BARBARELLA	Is your pet an Amazon? (Sorry, Jane).
BARKER	If he's loud, has his own game show, and can't keep his paws to himself
BARLEY	For a pet that likes soup
BARNABY	Perfect for a bloodhound
BARNABY JONES	For a dog detective, or a basset hound whose specialty is hunting
BARNETT	A Pyrenees sheepdog ... Also the name of a dentist I know that does root canals for a living (Yuck!!!).
BARNEY	Any purple dinosaur will do
BARNUM	Pair with Bailey
BARON	A pet with no hair
BARONESS	For a very feminine and regal pet ... with no hair

BARRIO BOY	For a pet from upper Manhattan
BARRY	For all of you Barry Manilow fans
BARTHOLOMARF	Bartholomew for a dog
BARTHOLOMEW	Bartholomew for a cat
BARTHOLOMOO	Bartholomew for a cow
BARTLEBY	English setter, English bulldog . . . or a fuzzy, furry cat
BARTÓK	For anyone who loves classical music
BASHA	For a Lhasa apso, Shih Tzu, Maltese, Pekingese
BASIL	For a pet that adds a little spice to your life
BASS MAN	A pet with a low growl
BASTILLE	For a pet you retrieve from the humane society
BATMAN	Double with Robin
BAXTER	A shorthaired Saint Bernard
BAYOU	For an American bloodhound
BAZAAR	A strange yet fashionable pet
BAZOOKA JOE	Perfect for a blowfish
BEA	A very homey, cozy name . . . something solid about it
BEACH BOY	A pet that can catch a Frisbee and chug a beer at the same time
BEANS	For a brown California spangled or any pet that's full of it
BEANSTOCK	For a tortoiseshell British shorthair, a very tall animal, or a climbing animal
BEAR	For a big, cuddly animal
BEARDSLEY	For an Old English sheepdog

BÉARNAISE	For a pup that likes a little sauce on his T-bone
BEASTIE BOY	For a Deutsche dogge or any other large guard-dog type
BEATRICE	For a little princess
BEAU	For a woman between husbands . . . a male pet
BEAUCHAMP	Pronounced "Beecham" . . . a great shopping street in London
BEAVER	Ward and June's son
BECKER	Remember Boris Becker?
BEDOUIN	For the pet that just can't stay in one place
BEDROCK	Fred Flintstone's hometown
BEEFEATER	For a harlequin Great Dane . . . no doubt it eats BEEF
BEEKER	A character on "Sesame Street," or a red-haired pet with big eyes
BEETHOVEN	For a pet that's hard of hearing
BEGUILER	The cat whose eyes can talk you into anything
BEIGE	For a beige pet
BELDING	For "Saved by the Bell" fans
BELLA	For a pretty Italian pet
BELLE	For a pretty French pet
BELLOW	For a loud American pet
BELUGA	For a pet with a taste of the finer things in life
BEN	For a gentle pet
BEN HUR	For someone who likes to drive chariots
BENJI	For a wirehaired fox terrier

BENJIE	Same
BENNY	For a small, gentle pet
BENSON	An animal that serves you
BENTLEY	For the Rolls-Royce of pets
BENTLY	Same
BERKELEY	For a radical pet
BERMUDA	For a tropical fish
BERNADETTE	For a vizsla ... intelligent, obedient, exceptional sense of smell
BERNADINE	For an airedale, Swedish dachsbracke, or small Swiss hound
BERNIE	An old Jewish pet that smokes cigars and goes to the track
BERRY	A pet for a Chuck
BERT	Pair with Ernie
BERTHA	For the biggest puppy in the litter
BERTIE	Goes to the track with Bernie
BERTRAM	For a bearded collie ... a herding breed with a joyous and affectionate personality
BESSIE	What else but a cow?
BETAMAX	For a pet that will soon be replaced
BETH	For a ''Rockford Files'' aficionado
BETSEY	Sounds like an active cat
BETSY	A dog difficult to housebreak (remember Betsy Wetsey?)
BETTE DAVIS	For a pug
BETTINA	For a Lapphund ... a Swedish dog, affectionate, patient with children, and distrustful of strangers
BETTY BOOP	For a Scottish fold

BEULAH	TV show of the same name (1950–53). Beulah was played by Ethel Waters and Louise Beavers.
BEVERLY	For a cat that likes to sit on sills
BIALY	See Bagel
BIANCA	The glamorous white mouse in *The Rescuers*
BIDDY	For a small card-playing pet
BIG BELLY	A basset hound that enjoys food just a little too much
BIG BERTHA	For a lilac point Himalayan or any of your oversize breeds
BIG BETTY	For any pet that works the counter at a truck stop
BIG BILL	For a very expensive breed
BIG BIRD	For a yellow parakeet
BIG EAR BOB	A rabbit's name
BIG EASY	For a New Orleans native
BIG MAC	Any large, imposing animal, or quite the opposite, small and petite
BIG SHOT	A pet with a Napoleon complex
BIG TONY	For a pet that makes you an offer you can't refuse
BIJAN	By appointment only
BILL	For someone with the "Wedding Bell Blues"
BILL BAILEY	Won't you come home . . . a pet that keeps wandering
BILL HICKOK	A pet that's always ready to be wild
BILLIE JEAN	For one of the retrievers . . . Chesapeake Bay, golden, Lab . . . any pet that goes after tennis balls

BILLMAR	For a bichon avanese, Labrador retriever, Chesapeake Bay retriever
BILLOW	A fluffy cat
BILLY DEE	For a border collie
BING	For a real crooner
BINGO	There was a farmer ...
BINKI	For a toy fox terrier, Yorkshire terrier, toy poodle, etcetera
BINZER	For a Yugoslavian mountain hound
BIONIC	For a very strong pet
BIRD DOG	For your hunting breeds
BIRDIE	A golfer's pet
BISCUIT	For a racehorse
BISHOP	A chess player's pet
BISQUE	For a fish
B.J.	For a basenji
BJORN	A tennis player's pet
BLACK BEANS	For a black pet with a lot of gas
BLACKBERRY	A black pet with a taste for fruit
BLACK FOOT	For a black and white Manx or any multi–colored pet with black paws
BLACKJACK	A gambler's pet, or a black Jack Russell terrier
BLACK MOON	A black pet with a white face
BLACK RUSSIAN	For a black pet with a taste for vodka
BLACK SMOKE	For a black smoke Oriental
BLACKWELL	For a pet with discerning taste in clothing
BLANCHE	For a ''Golden Girls'' fan with a white-haired pet, or for a *Streetcar* fan

BLANKET	For a lapcat
BLARNEY	For a pet that never tells the truth
BLEDSOE	For a chocolate shaded American shorthair
BLOCKER	For a rottweiler ... not too easy to get by him
BLONDIE	Dagwood's wife, Blondie Bumstead
BLOOD BROTHER	For someone who feels a very special affinity to their pet
BLOOM	A flowery or dainty cat
BLOOMER	For a puppy with enormous paws
BLOSSOM	I love this name for a pet
BLU	I love this name too
BLUE	Your favorite color, or a sad pet
BLUEBELL	For a blue Tonkinese, or any pet that's delicate and feminine
BLUEBERRY	For a sixties person who found his thrill on the hill
BLUE CHIP	A stock market investor's pet
BOB	For a American shorthair tabby
BOBBSEY	For twins
BOBBY BROWN	For any pet that likes to rap
BOBBY DARIN	For anyone who learned to dance to ''Mack the Knife''
BOBBY SHORT	Bulldog ... perfection in a voice
BOCA	For a parrot with a big mouth
BO DIDDLEY	For a sixties person who liked Bo Diddley
BODYGUARD	For a Yorkie or a doberman or a Costner ... whichever you fancy
BOGART	For a Clumber spaniel or a *Casablanca* fan. For pairs, see Bacall

BOGGS	For an animal that boggles the mind
BOGIE	And Bacall
BOÎTE DE BALL	For someone who loves France
BO JACKSON	For a big dog that runs fast
BOJANGLES	For a mister
BOLSHOI	Ballerina's big brother
BOLT	For a pet that keeps running away
BONBON	It has to be for a sweet little French poodle
BOND	As in James Bond. For an English foxhound
BONAPARTE	For a dog with jaws big enough to take the bone apart ... get it?
BONJOVI	A singer's pet
BONNIE	An Irish setter, Irish terrier, etcetera
BONNIE LASS	Also for any of the Irish breeds
BONO	For a pet that sings like a dream
BONSAI	For a dwarf pet
BOO	A pet that startles easily
BOOKER	A casting agent's pet
BOOMER	A pet for someone born after 1945
BOOTS	Boots is for dogs and Socks is for cats
BOOTSIE	If Socks is for cats and Boots is for dogs, then Bootsie is for a wootsie dog
BORAX	For someone who loves to clean
BOREALIS	For a stargazer
BORG	Tennis anyone?
BORGIA	Lucrezia

BORIS	For any of the Russian breeds ... wolfhound, borzoi, etcetera
BORIS BADENOV	Pair with Natasha Fatale
BORSCHT	Again, Russian wolfhound, borzoi, Russian blue
BOSCO	A favorite chocolate syrup to make chocolate milk
BOSH	For a small Continental spaniel
BOSLEY	A "Charlie's Angels" fan
BOSS	A Springsteen fan
BOSWELL	For a rough-coated Bohemian pointer. A hunting dog from Bohemia, and aristocratic to boot
BOTTICELLI	For a fleshy pet
BOUILLABAISSE	A good name for the entire fish tank
BOUNCER	For a pug or a Yorkshire terrier
BOURGUIGNON	For a French meat eater
BOWERY BOYS	One of my favorite TV shows growing up
BOWSER	For a bloodhound
BOXER	Any pet that comes home with a few too many bruises
BOXY	For a Scottish terrier
BOYCHICK	For one of those Easter chicks that you eventually have to give away once they start cock-a-doodling
BOYD	For a bichon frise
BOY SCOUT	For a goody-goody
BOY WONDER	For a robin
BOZETTE	Bozo's girlfriend
BOZO	Bozette's boyfriend

BOZWELL	For a Maltese, cockatoo, or red Oriental
BRADLEY	For a Cairn terrier, cocker spaniel, English springer spaniel
BRAHMS	A composer's pet, or a pet that sleeps a lot
BRANCUSI	For an Italian hound . . . a vivacious, robust hunter
BRANDO	For a pet that knows how to tango
BRANDON	90210
BRANDY	There are an awful lot of Brandys. I don't know why.
BRAWLER	Boxer's *compadre*
BRENDON	Not quite 90210. This name literally means stinking hair.
BRIDGE	For a pet that makes peace in the family
BRIDIE	For an Irish setter, Irish terrier, or Irish water spaniel
BRIE	Another name that would go with Baguette, or for a standard poodle
BRIGITTE	Loves Bernie
BRILLIANT	For a very colorful pet
BRINKER	For a Brinks truck guard
BRINKS	For a guard dog
BRIOCHE	For someone into the comfort of their breakfast
BRISTOL	For a prickly pet
BROADHURST	A theater goer's pet
BROADWAY JOE	For a Monday morning quarterback
BRODERICK	For an Old English sheepdog
BRODIE	For a pet in its prime (Miss Jean)

BROKER	An insurance agent's pet
BROMLEY	A skier's pet
BRONCO	For your larger breeds
BRONSON	For someone who takes care of his family
BROWNIE	One of the all-time favorite pet names
BROWNING	For a pet that's not quite toast yet, or an Elizabeth Barrett fan
BROWN SUGAR	For a brown classic tabby
BROWSER	A pet that likes to window-shop
BRUCE	For a very pensive goldfish
BRUNHILDE	For a real work dog, or a Wagner lover
BRUNO	For a German wirehaired pointer
BRUTIS	A pet that you feel might eventually, and surprisingly, betray you
BRYANT	For a pet that gumbles, uh, grumbles
BRYNNER	For a bald pet with a good sense of drama
BUBBA	For a linebacker, or a bullmastiff
BUBBLES	Another fish name
BUBELEH	Yiddish for sweetheart
BUBKES	Yiddish for peanuts
BUCCELLATI	For a jewelry freak
BUCKINGHAM	For an English bulldog
BUCKWHEAT	A pet with hair that stands straight up (Cane Nudo)
BUDDY	Sally's pal from ''The Dick Van Dyke Show''
BUFFALO BILL	A pet that just can't seem to win the Super Bowl
BUFFALO BOB	Howdy Doody pal

BUFFET	A pet that constantly eats
BUFFY	From the show "Family Affair"
BUGATTI	For a foreign car enthusiast
BULFINCH	For someone into mythology
BULGARI	A name for someone who loves jewelry and doesn't mind overpaying
BULLET	The Wonder Dog . . . Roy Rogers
BULLWINKLE	If you have a moose, or pair with Rocket J. Squirrel (that's Rocky!)
BUMPERS	For a dog that catches the car and hits the bumpers
BUMSTEAD	For Blondie and Dagwood fans
BUNKO	For someone into fraud
BUNNY	For a chinchilla Persian
BUNYAN	For a Paul fan, or has problem feet
BURBANK	For a pet that loves to watch game shows
BURGESS	For a beagle
BUSTER	For a crab, or a Brown
BUSTER BROWN	A dog that likes to live in shoes
BUTCH	For a sexually ambivalent pet
BUTCH CASSIDY	For someone into cowboys or bank and train robberies
BUTLER	He, definitely, did it
BUTTER	For a cream point Himalayan
BUTTERCUP	A female bulldog
BUTTERSCOTCH	For a golden Persian
BUTTON	A pet with one spot on it
BUTTONS	A dalmatian
BUZZIE	"Leave It to Beaver"

BUZZY   A drinker's pet

BYBLOS   For a blue Tonkinese into good clothing

BYRD   Good for a bird!

BYRON   A pet that has a sense of intellectual superiority

C. S. LEWIS	For someone into literature
C3PO	*Star Wars* fan
CAB	For someone who's always in taxis
CABALLERO	A Spanish cowboy
CABBAGE PATCH	For a lilac lynx point colorpoint exotic
CABBAGE ROSE	For a red Abyssinian
CABBIE	A New Yorker's pet
CABERNET	A wine lover's pet
CABIN FEVER	For an indoor pet
CABLE	A television watcher's pet
CABOT	For a wirehaired pointing griffon ... cute, wiry, lively, tallish, and intelligent
CAESAR	A salad eater's pet
CAFÉ AU LAIT	For a black and white
CAGNEY	For a James fan
CAINE	For a kung fu expert
CAIRO	For an Egyptian pet, or a Middle East aficionado
CAKE	For a bichon frise

CALAMITY JANE	For an animal that bumps into things
CALCULATOR	A very cunning pet
CALDER	A sculptor's pet
CALDWELL	Another name for an art lover
CALEB	For a bronze Egyptian mau
CALENDAR GIRL	For a pinup pet
CALHOUN	For an Irish setter
CALI or CALLIE	A blue classic tabby or British shorthair or a red classic tabby British shorthair
CALIFORNIA DREAMIN'	For a displaced Californian
CALLAHAN	For an Irish wolfhound
CALLOWAY	For a jazz fan
CALVIN	For an English cocker spaniel, or someone into cotton underwear
CALZONE	For someone into Italian food
CAMARO	For a Chevy fan
CAMBER	For an Iceland dog . . . lively, active, and likes to eat fish
CAMBRIDGE	For an anglophile or a Harvard grad
CAMDEN	For a Norwich terrier . . . one of the smallest terriers
CAMELOT	For a person who remembers the sixties
CAMERA	A photographer's pet
CAMERON	Always makes me think of John Swazey
CAMI	For a Norwegian elkhound . . . specializes in hunting elk
CAMILLE	For a very dramatic pet

CAMP	For a pet that's really "in"
CAMPAIGN	A political pet
CAMPBELL	For someone into canned food
CAMPER	For a very outdoorsy pet
CAMUS	For a very intellectual pet
CANCEL	For a very angry pet
CANDICE	For a very Murphy pet
CANDIDE	Voltaire's novel, published in 1759
CANDY	For a very sweet pet
CANNES	A movie critic's pet
CANON	For a copycat
CAPER	For a James Bondian pet
CAPONE	For a gangster pet, one that knows how to keep the neighborhood in toe
CAPOTE	For a true-man pet
CAPPUCCINO	For an Italian hyperactive pet
CAPPY	For a Bedlington terrier
CAPRA	For someone who likes romantic comedies
CAPTAIN	For a courageous pet
CAPTAIN HOOK	A three-legged pet
CAPTAIN KANGAROO	An animal that wakes up at eight A.M.
CAPTAIN VIDEO	A pet that watches TV a lot
CARAMEL	For a cream classic tabby
CARAMEL CUSTARD	For a cream classic tabby
CARBONARA	For a saucy pet

CAR 54	For the pet that you have to keep saying "WHERE ARE YOU?" to
CARL	Carl the rottweiler of children's book fame
CARLISLE	For someone who sells clothing from their home or is into British writers
CARLITO	For someone who likes to get his way
CARLOS	For a Labrador retriever, French poodle, or Portuguese water dog ... depending if you want to be outrageous
CARLOTTA	For a pretty dog with a Mediterranean flair
CARLTON	A smoker's pet
CARLY	For a cat that loves to sing and write songs
CARMEL	A California dreamer
CARMEN	An opera lover's pet
CARMICHAEL	Hoagy
CARMINE	For anyone who owns an Italian restaurant
CARNEGIE	For a pet that likes sleeping in a hall
CAROL	"Oh, Carol" ... anyone who feels like a fool
CARPOOL	For any suburban parent
CARRERA	For someone who likes sunglasses ... or Porsches
CARRINGTON	A pet for a "Dynasty" fan
CARSON	For someone who misses Johnny
CARSTAIRS	A butler wanna be
CARTER	A pet with lust in his heart, or your favorite "ER" guy
CARTIER	For a jewel of a pet

CARTWRIGHT	A pet for anyone named Adam, Hoss, Little Joe, or Pa
CARUSO	For a pet with big lungs and a need to sing
CASABLANCA	A pet for someone who lives in a white house
CASBAH	For a "rockin' " pet
CASEY	For an American shorthair
CASHMERE	For a soft, furry pet
CASINO	A gambler's pet
CASPER	For a vanishing dog
CASPURR	For a vanishing cat
CASSANDRA	For a very fancy, fluffy Persian cat
CASSATT	American impressionist
CASSIDY	For any animal that hops along
CASSIE	For an American shorthair (or longhair)
CASSIUS	For a pet with feet of clay
CASTANETS	For a cat that dances flamenco
CAT	For a lazy namer, or a fan of *Breakfast at Tiffany's*
CATALINE	For a creative namer
CAVIAR	For a Persian cat, or a cat with a lot of class
CB	For someone who doesn't have a car phone yet
CBS	For someone into TV . . . triple with ABC and NBC
CD	For someone into music discs
CECIL	For an English springer spaniel
CECILIA	For a pet who's "breakin' your heart"

CEDRIC	I love this name. A Great Dane would be fabulous.
CEE CEE	For a "rider." Are you into R&B?
CELESTE	For a heavenly pet
CELIA	For a seal
CELLO	For a big, fat, oversize pet
CERUTTI	Fine children's clothes
CÉZANNE	A painter's pet
CHA-CHA	For a dancing pet
CHACHI	For a "Happy Days" fan
CHAGALL	Another artist's pet name
CHAMBERLAIN	For an English bulldog
CHAMP	For a boxer
CHAMPAGNE	For a bubbly pet
CHANCELLOR	For a diplomatic pet
CHANEL	For a pet that smells good and dresses well
CHANG	For a Tibetan terrier or a Chinese temple dog
CHANNEL	For someone who can't stay on one TV channel for more than ten minutes
CHANNING	A skinny pet with big lips and a loud voice
CHAPSTICK	For someone named Suzy, or someone with problem lips
CHARCOAL	For a black smoke American shorthair
CHARDONNAY	Kathie Lee's bichon
CHARGER	A shopper's pet
CHARLA	For a chestnut Angora
CHARLEMAGNE	For a French pointer
CHARLES	Formal (*see* "Chuck")
CHARLEY	For an American bloodhound

CHARLIE	For any *Peanuts* cartoon strip fan
CHARLIE BROWN	Snoopy's pal
CHARLIE CHAN	For a Chinese crested dog detective
CHARLIE'S ANGEL	An angel for a Charlie
CHARLOTTE	For a spider
CHARMER	For a Don Juan
CHARMING	For a prince
CHARMSIE	For a princess
CHARO	For a busty songbird
CHASE	For a lover of American Impressionism
CHASER	For a dog that runs after cars
CHATZUK	For a cinnamon Javanese
CHAUCER	For an English setter, English bulldog, or English springer spaniel
CHAUNCEY	For an irish blue Terrier, Irish setter, or Irish water spaniel
CHAUNCY	same
CHECKERS	See "Nixon"
CHEERIOS	For the cereal lover
CHEERS	For a drinking pet
CHEESECAKE	For the cheesecake lover
CHEEVER	For an under or an over
CHEKHOV	For a Russian wolfhound or borzoi
CHELSEA	For any of the British breeds ... Old English sheepdog, Yorkshire terrier, or English bulldog
CHELSEY	For a tortie and white Scottish fold
CHER	For a multitalented pet with a predilection for dressing way out there

CHEROKEE	For someone into Indian names
CHESSIE	Nice for a Chesapeake Bay retriever
CHESTER	A big, brown dog
CHESTNUT	For a horse. Also, a hair color (the actual name of the color on the bottle).
CHEWBACCA	*Star Wars*
CHI CHI	Little, teeny-weeny pets
CHICO	Perfect for a Mexican hairless or a Chihuahua
CHIEF	For a giant schnauzer . . . large, steady watchdog and bodyguard
CHIFFON	For a blue-cream point Himalayan
CHILI	For a hot pet
CHILI PEPPER	For a cinnamon Javanese
CHILL	For a hyper pet
CHIPPER	For a happy pet
CHLOË	A designer's pet
CHOCK FULL OF NUTS	For a crazy, hyperactive pet
CHOCOLATE	For a brown pet
CHOCOLATE CHIP	For a brown and black pet
CHOCOLATE MALT	For a brown and beige pet
CHOCOLATE MOUSSE	For a pudgy, soft, brown pet
CHOPIN	A musician's pet
CHOPPER	A pet with big teeth
CHOPSTICK	For those people who always insist on chopsticks

CHOP SUEY	For any of the Chinese breeds ... Lhasa apso, Shih Tzu, blue Tonkinese, etcetera
CHOWDER	A name for a clam
CHOW MEIN	Perfect for a chow chow
CHRISSY	From "Three's Company"
CHRISTIE	Sotheby's competition
CHROMIUM	A pet for someone in the metal finishing business or the owner of a silver-gray pet
CHUCK	For an informal King Charles spaniel
CHUNK	A fat cat
CHURCHILL	A bulldog with a cigar
CHUTNEY	For a golden Persian
CHUTZPAH	Yiddish for a pet with no inhibitions
CINDERELLA	For a swan
CINDERFELLA	For a Jerry Lewis fan
CINDY	Cinderella's nickname
CINNAMON	Choice for the cinnamon Javanese
CISSY	Another name for those hard-to-housebreak pets
CLAIRE	For someone who loves pastry and doesn't like to be hit over the head with it ... short for eclair
CLANCY	A police dog
CLAPTON	A guitarist's pet
CLARA	For a Bernese mountain dog ... very big but energetic and loyal
CLARA BARTON	A shaded silver American shorthair
CLARABELL	From the "Howdy Doody" show
CLARANCE	Any pet that knows how to use its paws

CLARENCE	same as Clarance
CLARISSA	For a pet pig or cow
CLARK	For someone named Lois
CLARKE	For someone who hangs out in bars (Clark bars)
CLARK KENT	A quick change artist's pet
CLASSIC	For a golfer
CLAUDE	For a French spaniel
CLAUDIO	For an Italian pointer
CLAYTON	An American Staffordshire terrier
CLEO	The basset hound on "The People's Choice"
CLEOPATRA	For a pet that has total self-confidence and possibly a touch of grandiosity
CLERGY	For a cat with a white neck
CLIFF	A postman's pet
CLIFFORD	For a weimaraner ... affectionate and tends to be stubborn
CLIVE	For someone in the music business
CLOCKWORK	For a very bizarre orange tabby
CLOONEY	A pet for a Rosemary or a George
CLORIS	Mary Tyler Moore's neighbor
CLOROX	A bleached blonde's pet
CLOUD	For a very fluffy, white cat
CLOVER	For a crimson pet
CLUE	For a game player
CLYDE	Bonnie's cohort
COACH	An athlete's pet
COBRA	For a pit bull
COCHISE	For a pet that likes to wear feathers

COCKTAIL	For a pet that comes to life after five o'clock
COCO	Perfection for a chocolate poodle
CODY	A pet for a Kathie Lee fan
COKE	*See* "Doubles," Pepsi
COLA	For a bubbly pet
COLETTE	A French poodle or a French bulldog
COLLECTOR	For a pet that picks up strays and brings them home
COLLEEN	For an Irish setter
COLIN	Another Irish setter name
COLONEL KLINK	A pet for a "Hogan's Heroes" fan
COLONEL POTTER	A pet for a "M*A*S*H" fan
COLORADO	A skier's pet
COLT	For your larger, lean breeds
COLUMBO	A detective's pet, or a yogurt fan
COLUMBUS	An adventurous pet
COMANCHE	For a wild pet
COMATOSE	For a listless pet
COMBINATION	Good for a mutt
COMPTON	For a know-it-all
COMSTOCK	For a basset hound
CONCHITTA	For a Chihuahua
CONDOR	For a Doberman pinscher
CONFETTI	For a pet born on New Year's Eve
CONGRESSMAN	A politician's pet
CONNECTICUT YANKEE	For a pet from New England
CONNOR	For an Australian terrier

CONNORS	A Jimmy fan
CONRAD	For a pet that will only stay at a Hilton
CONSTABLE	A serious pet that walks the grounds
CONSTANCE	His mate
CONSTANTINE	For a Greek pet
CONSUELA	Long-haired Saint Bernard
CONTESSA	For a very fancy pet
COOPER	For a Gary fan
COORS	A beer drinker's pet
COPACABANA	For someone named Rico
CORA	Smooth fox terrier
CORAL	For a calico American wirehair
CORAZÓN	Heart, in Spanish
CORBETT	For a great spitz
CORDUROY	A striped pet
CORINA	A blue and white Maine coon
CORINNA CORINNA	I love you so
CORKY	For a "Murphy Brown" fan
CORNELIA	A female briard
CORNELIUS	A male briard . . . a wonderful name, actually. I like it for anything.
CORNY	For a pet that tells bad jokes
COROT	Artist
CORPORATE	A pet for someone who works at IBM
CORTEZ	One very cool dude
CORY	A pet that likes to eat your leftovers
COSBY	For a pet that is very funny
COSMO	For someone who loved "Topper"

COSMOS	For someone who loves the planets
COSTA	A tough, manly pet
CÔTE D'AZUR	For someone who loves the south of France
COTTAGE CHEESE	For someone who loves to diet
COUNSELOR	A pet for someone who's always solving other people's problems
COUNT BASIE	A very mellow, contented animal
COUNTESS	For a very regal pet
COUSTEAU	For your favorite fish
COWBOY	For a Jack Russell terrier with a bandanna around his neck
COWGIRL	For a female Jack Russell terrier with a bandanna around her neck
CRACKER JACK	Another favorite name for a Jack Russell
CRACKERS	For a pet with a screw loose, or for Polly, of course
CRACKLIN' ROSE	For a very old, wrinkled rose
CRAIG	For a Scottish terrier
CRAMER	For a flat-coated retriever . . . looks like a Newfoundland, obedient and affectionate
CRANBERRY	For a red, squishy pet
CRAZY EDDIE	For a pet into electronics . . . that occasionally gets itself into big trouble
CREAM	The real thing
CREATOR	For a pet that creates havoc
CRÈME CARAMEL	For a cream tabby point Devon rex
CRÈME DE COCO	For a chocolate tortie Burmese

CREMORA	A substitute pet
CROCKETT	For a coonhound, Chesapeake Bay retriever, or any of the hunting breeds
CROISSANT	For a French poodle, French bulldog, or French spaniel
CROMWELL	For a Gordon setter . . . Scottish, intelligent, and less active than other setters
CROONER	For someone who loves music
CROUTON	A salad eater's pet
CRUISER	Definitely for a nonneutered male pet
CRUNCH	English bulldog
CRUSADER	For a pet with a cause
CUCUMBER	A shorthaired dachshund
CUDDLES	Old English sheepdog . . . unless, of course, snakes are your thing
CUJO	For someone into Stephen King
CUPCAKE	A rottweiler, golden Persian, Welsh corgi, or whatever strikes your fancy
CUPID	A matchmaker's pet
CURLY	*See* "Triples," Moe and Larry's pal
CUSTARD	For a person with a sweet tooth
CUSTER	A pet that likes to do battle
CUSTER'S LAST STAND	The last of the litter
CUTIE PIE	A bichon frise. What could be cuter?
CUTLER	A rough-coated Collie. This is the "Lassie" dog, robust, active, and intelligent.
CYRANO	A dog with a long nose. A borzoi comes to mind, or a dachshund.
CYRIL	A basset hound. They have such personality.

DADA	For the big daddy of breeds
DAFFNEY	For a blue-cream point Himalayan
DAFFODIL	For a Westphalian basset, Scottish terrier, or chow chow
DAFFY	If you have a duck, you're in luck
DA GAMA	For someone who likes sailing the seven seas
DAGMAR	A Swedish elkhound . . . and, I remember *I Remember Mama*
DAGWOOD	See "Doubles," Blondie's husband
DAILY DOUBLE	A gambler's pet
DAILY NEWS	A dog that's paper trained
DAILY TIMES	A discerning dog that's paper trained
DAISHI	A dashing Shih Tzu
DAISY	Perfect for a standard poodle
DAKOTA	For an Afghan with a cowboy scarf around its neck
DALE	A pet for a Roy Rogers fan
DALE EVANS	For an even more avid Roy Rogers fan
DALÍ	A painter's pet

DALLAS   A pet for either a cheerleader or a football fan

D'AMATO   A political pet

DAME   A tough broad

DAMIAN   For a rottweiler, Deutsche dogge, doberman, etcetera

DAMIEN   What an omen (a pet from hell)

DAMON   A boxer, great spitz, or Pomeranian

DAMSEL   For a pet constantly in distress

DANBURY   For a pet from Connecticut

DANCER   Great for a reindeer or a dancer

DANDEE   For a positively positive pet

DANDY   A Dandie Dinmont terrier

DANDY DAN   Someone into sixties music

DANETTE   A female Dan

DANIEL BOONE   For anyone into coonskin hats

DANIELLE   For a pet made of Steele

DANISH   A chubby pet

DANNY BOY   For any Irish pet

DAN RIVER   For a pet that likes to sleep in your sheets

DANTE   For a Doberman pinscher

DAPHNE   One of the very feminine names

DAPPER   For a Dan, or a well dressed pooch

DARBERT   For a Norsk buhund . . . of Norwegian descent, courageous and energetic

DARBY   For an Irish blue terrier, Irish setter, or Derby with an accent

DARE   Great for a daredevil pet

DAREN	For a bearded collie ... very cute looking, fairly large, a lot of fun, and likes to sleep outside
DARIA	For someone into finance
DARIAN LAMB	For a pet that knows how to make "tracks"
DARIEN	Another Connecticut pet
DARIN or DARREN	Another spelling for a bearded collie, or a pet that's simply "Bewitched"
DARK CHOCOLATE	For a black American curl
DARLENE	One of the Mouseketeers
DARLING	Peter Pan ... Wendy's last name
DARNEL	For a Tennessee treeing brindle (that's a dog, really)
DARRYL	Darryl's other brother
D'ARTAGNAN	One of the Three Musketeers
DARTER	A mouse in the house
DARTH VADER	A big black dog that carries a light saber
DARWIN	A great name for a monkey
DASH	For a greyhound or other racing type of pet
D.A.T.	For someone in music
DATA	For a computer buff
DATABASE	For a pet that keeps track of the family
DATO	For a Japanese spitz. Bold and happy but suspicious of strangers.
DAVIS	For a border collie
DAVY	For any of the American breeds ... also, parrots and gerbils

DAVY CROCKETT	For someone into coonskin hats
DAWN	For a pet rooster
DAYTONA BEACH	A car racer's pet . . . also a pet found during spring break
DAZZLE	For a real crowd pleaser
DEAN	For someone who likes school
DEBUSSY	For someone who likes music
DECKER	For someone who likes boxers
DECORATOR	For a pet that leaves new ''items'' around the house
DEE DEE	For a Dandie Dinmont terrier
DEEJAY	For a pet that's always talking
DEGAS	A painter's pet
DELBERT	For a shorthaired dachshund
DELIA	A card player's pet
DELICACY	For an Italian pet that loves to eat
DELICIOUS	For an American pet that loves to eat
DELILAH	For a pet that's into grooming
DELLA	For a pet that likes to go out in the street, or an owner who watches ''Perry Mason'' reruns
DELMAN	For a person with a shoe fetish
DELMONICO	For a person that likes the best restaurants, or red meat
DEL MONTE	For a pet that eats canned food
DELORES	For a chocolate tortie Burmese
DELTA	It's a bird (it's a plane)
DELTA BLUE	A bluebird
DELTA DAWN	An early bird

DEMERIT	For a pet that's always in the principal's office
DEMI	For someone who wants Moore
DEMITASSE	For a Yorkie or any of the mini breeds
DEMO	For a pet always having to prove itself
DEMOLITION	For a big, clumsy pet
DEMPSEY	Another Jack Russell name . . . or for a boxer
DE NIRO	For someone who likes Robert
DENISE	Shubi doo, I'm in love with youoo, Denise, shubi doo
DENNIS THE MENACE	For a perfectly lovely looking pet that wreaks havoc
DENVER	For someone who likes both the city and the singer
DEPP	For a Johnny come lately
DEPUTY	For a pet that prowls the house
DEPUTY DAWG	The cartoon detective from the sixties
DERBY	For a pet from Kentucky
DESDEMONA	Will live longer if not paired with Othello
DESI	*See* ''Doubles,'' for a Lucy fan
DESIGNER	For a pet that makes plans in advance
DESIRE	For that seductive pet
DESIREE	For a Welsh corgi . . . lively and affectionate
DESMOND	For a Scottish terrier . . . lively, independent, and devoted to the family
DESMON TOO TOO	So much more clever than the II
DE SOTO	For a pet soon to be obsolete

DESPERADO	For someone into cowboy movies
DESTIMONA	A lilac point Himalayan or a blue-cream point Himalayan
DETOUR	For the puppy that never comes home in time
DEVINA	For a divine Italian pet
DEVON	For an English setter, English springer spaniel, English bulldog, etcetera
DEVONSHIRE	For an English cocker spaniel (or all the rest)
DIABLO	For a devil
DIAMOND	For your gem
DIAMOND JIM	A rich pet, or an expensive one
DIAMONDS	For a golden Persian
DICK	See Dick, see Dick run
DICKENS	For a pet that likes to creep up on you and scare the dickens out of you
DICK TRACY	For a bloodhound or coonhound
DIEGO	Don Diego. Remember Zorro?
DIET	A Weight Watcher's pet
DIETER	A pet that's a finicky eater
DIETRICH	Marlene
DIJON	For a mustard lover
DILETTANTE	For a pet that does nothing but eat and sleep
DILLINGER	For a gun toter . . . any of the guard dogs . . . or for a cockatiel
DILLY	For a real winner . . . but what a cute name
DIMITRI	For a Greek hound
DIMITRIUS	For another Greek pet
DIMPLES	Any pet with spots, or a snake

DINA	For a salamander or a chameleon
DINAH	For a pet that will "See the USA in a Chevrolet"
DINGER	A pet that keeps bumping into the family car
DINO	Fred Flintstone's pet, or someone who likes Dean Martin
DION	Head of The Belmonts
DIPLOMAT	For a pet that won't take sides
DIPSEY DOODLE	For a red Abyssinian that turns itself inside out
DIRK	This is a name that is very masculine and would seem to be appropriate for any macho pet
DIRTY HARRY	A pet that takes the law into its own hands
DISCO	A seventies pet
DISCOVER	For a pet constantly digging in the yard
DISNEY	For a pet with good family values
DITA	For a ferret
DITTO	For a parrot
DIVINE	Remember Andy Divine?
DIXIE	For a southern belle ... maybe a rabbit?
DIXIE CUP	For a chihuahua
DIZZY	For a trumpet player
DOC	A nurse's pet
DODGER	For a pet that runs away when you try to get it
DOLAN	For a basset hound
DOLBY	For a dog that barks in stereo

DOLLAR BILL	For a hawk, or a material boy
DOLLY	For a sweet, big-busted pet
DOLORES	For a Maine coon or maybe better for a mixed breed
DOMANI	For an Italian greyhound who puts things off till tomorrow
DOMINGO	For a Spanish mastiff who puts things off till Sunday
DOMINIC	For an Italian hound
DOMINIQUE	For a French bulldog
DOMINO	Dalmatian
DOM PERIGNON	For a pet with a taste for the finer things in life
DONAHUE	For a person named Phil
DONALD	For a bridge-playing person in real estate, or for a duck
DONATELLO	For a black silver mackerel tabby European shorthair
DON CORLEONE	A pet for anyone who liked *The Godfather*
DON DIEGO	A pet for anyone who liked *Zorro*
DON JUAN	For a very sexy pet
DONNA	Wouldn't this be a great name for a female mixed breed?
DONOVAN	For a mellow yellow pet
DON QUIXOTE	For a very confused pet
DONUT	For a round, jolly pet
DOODLE	For a slow paced pet with a short attention span
DOOGIE	A pet that aspires to medical school at a young age
DOOLEY	A dog that hangs his head, or for a person named Tom

DOOLITTLE	For a lazy pet, or one that talks to other animals
DOONEY	Burke's brother
DOORMAN	A concierge's pet
DORA	A good guinea pig name
DOREEN	An Irish water spaniel
DORIAN	For a gray pet
DORIAN GRAY	For a pet that gets younger
DORIS	Perfect for a cat of mixed breed
DORKIS	For a goofy pet
DOROTHY	For anyone moving from Kansas
DORSET	A wonderful town in Vermont
DOSTOEVSKY	Another one for any of your Russian breeds
DOT	For a tiny animal
DOTTS	For a leopard
DOTTY	For a dalmatian
DOUBLEDAY	An avid reader's pet
DOUGH BOY	You poke it in the stomach and it giggles.
DOUGLAS	A very proper name
DOW JONES	A pet for someone who likes to follow the market
DOWNHILL	A skier's pet
DOWNTOWN	A dude's pet
DOWRY	For an extremely expensive pet
DOW WOW	Please don't name your dog this
DOZER	For a cat-naper
DR. LIVINGSTON	Presumably a pet
DR. SEUSS	For a cat in a hat

DR. STRANGELOVE	For a Stanley Kubrick fan, or for a pet that keeps nipping at you
DRACULA	For a bat or a doberman
DRAGON	For a pet with a limp
DRAKE	Paul from "Perry Mason"
DRAMA	For a melodramatic pet
DRAPER	For a person who hangs curtains
DRAWERS	For a cat that gets into everything
DREAMER	*See* Don Quixote
DREYFUSS	The dog on "Empty Nest"
DROOPY	A cartoon dog—perfect for a bassett hound
DRUMMER	For a Clumber spaniel
DRUMMOND	For a very rich city pet
DUANE	A southern pet
DUBUFFET	A painter's pet
DUCHESS	For a pet with high aspirations
DUCKIE	A character from the movie *Pretty in Pink*
DUDE	For one cool pet
DUDLEY	Wonderful name for any breed
DUFFY	For a golden retriever
DUFY	An artist's pet
DUKE	For a pug
DUKE OF EARL	I see this for a Great Dane because they are so regal.
DULCINEA	Don Quixote's love interest
DUMBO	For a pet with big ears
DUMPLING	For a chubby little thing
DUN	Bradstreet's brother
DUNBAR	For a tawny Great Dane

DUNHILL	For a pet that lights up your life
DUNLOP	A tennis player's pet
DURAN DURAN	For a singing pet
DURANTE	For a pet with a large nose, or a parrot in particular
DURBAN	For a South African pet
DUSHANE	A border collie
DUSTIN	For the owner who cleans the far recesses of the closets
DUSTY	For a cat that goes into the far recesses of the closets
DUTCH	A great name for any dog
DUTCH BOY	A painter's pet
DUTCH GIRL	A cleaner's pet
DVOŘÁK	Composer
DWEEZIL	For the son of a rock and roll star
DWINDELL	For a Chinese Shar-pei ... as they get larger, their wrinkles dwindle
DYLAN	For a pet that whines or for a Thomas
DYNAMO	For a pet that just never stops
DYNAMITE	For a hyperactive pet

E. T.	A pug, or any animal that calls home often
EAGAN	For a basset griffon vendéen . . . courageous, tenacious, and lovable
EAMES	Has good taste in chairs
EARFUL	For a parrot
EARHART	A bird (for obvious reasons)
EARL	Wouldn't this be a great name for any dog?
EARL GREY	A tea lover's pet
EARLY	For a preemie
EARNEST	For a pleaser
EARTHA	For a person into kits
EARTHY	Nice excuse for your mixed breed
EASTER	Bunnies that work once a year
EASTERN	Geographically flexible
EASTON	For a blue silver patched tabby Maine coon . . . nice, amiable temperament
EASTWOOD	For a gun totin' pet
EASY	Already housebroken, neutered, and doesn't shed

EASY CHAIR	Where you find it every time you come home
EASY RIDER	Pet horse or Newfoundland
EASY STREET	You won the lottery and now that you no longer have to work, you can have a pet
EASY WAY	For the pet that goes in and out of the trap door in your house
EBENEZER	For a pet that won't share
EBERT	A pet that likes movies and is all thumbs
EBONY	A black shorthair
ECCENTRIC	A cane nudo or a Chinese crested dog (no hair except for a tuft on its head)
ECHO	For a parrot
ECLAIR	For a cream puff of a pet
ECLIPSE	For a pet with a black and white face
ECOLOGY	For a pet that cares about the environment
ECRU	Cream mackerel tabby, seal lynx shorthair, blond cocker spaniel, or a pet that resembles the color
ECSTASY	Intimidating for the people in your life
EDDIE	For a fan of ''Frasier''
EDEN	Garden snakes
EDEN ROC	Another Miami memory
EDGAR	Will make people smile, unless you insist it's after Poe
EDGE	For a highly neurotic pet
EDISON	For a con man

EDITH	Whining voice . . . pair with Archie, or for a nice, big, fat, good-natured, lilac point Himalayan
EDITH WHARTON	Strong, female, American born
EDMUND	Old English sheepdogs, bulldogs, etcetera
EDNA	Great cat name
EDO	For a Japanese bobtail
EDSEL	For a pet that goes out of style
EDWARD	A pedigree that falls in love with a divorced commoner
EDWARDS	You bought a lot of goldfish at once but can't tell them apart
EDWEENA	Born old and female
EDWIN	Born old and male
EENY MEENY	Good for collections of small things . . . Teeny Weeny, Itsy Bitsy, Miney and Mo
EEYORE	Resembles a donkey . . . think Winnie the Pooh and Piglet
EFREM	Nostalgia for "77 Sunset Strip" and "The F.B.I."
EGAD	You've never gotten over what it looks like
EGAN	For an Irish setter . . . energetic and full of feeling
EGBERT	May make people smile, but at your pet's expense
EGG CREAM	Perfect for a yellow Labrador retriever
EGGHEAD	Actually, not very nice
EGGNOG	A Christmas pet
EGGROLL	A Chinese Shar-pei

EGO	You fell in love because it looked exactly like you
EGYPT	An Egyptian mau, sphynx, or other particularly exotic animal
EIDERDOWN	Angoras, Persians, Maine coons, sheepdogs, afghans, and, of course, ducks
EIFFEL	French poodle or French bulldog
8 1/2	Maybe it's the markings, maybe it's the life expectancy, or maybe it's fat and reminds you of Fellini
EINSTEIN	Any animal with long white hair. The genius part will be taken for granted.
EISENHOWER	A nice pet, partial to retrieving golf balls
EKG	For a hyperactive pet
ELAM	Persians
ÉLAN	For a pet with style
ELBA	For someone from an island
EL CID	For a Spanish mastiff
ELDERBERRY	Berry's grandparent
EL DORADO	A fish with large fins
ELDRIDGE	For a jailbird
ELEANOR	An independent companion with large teeth
ELECTRA	An avenging pet. Guard dogs
ELECTRIC	Luminous fish
ELF	For a very small pet
EL GRECO	For a Spanish greyhound
ELIJAH	For a pet that drinks from a cup when you're not looking
ELIOT NESS	For a guard dog

ELISHA	A pet that particularly likes a walk with the leash
ELIZABETH	English sheepdogs, English bulldogs, etcetera whose offspring are trouble
ELKE	For a Swedish elkhound
ELLEN	Not quite Helen . . . French bulldog
ELLERY	For a queen
ELLIE	Elizabeth's nickname
ELLINGTON	A duke's pet
ELLIOT	Makes the pet sound smart
ELLIPSIS	Dalmatians
ELLIS	For a pet from an island
ELLSWORTH	For a very formal pet
ELLY MAY	A Beverly Hillbilly
ELMER	The result of inbreeding
ELMER FUDD	Basset hound . . . anything with big ears
ELMIRA	Skinny black cats
ELOISE	The Pekingese
ELOPE	Romantic cats partial to ladders
ELROY	More dignified than the last Roy you owned
ELSA	Heroine of Wagner's *Lohengrin*
ELSIE	Either you have a cow, or it reminds you of one
ELSINORE	Great Danes
ELTON	A smooth fox terrier
ELTON JOHN	For an English bulldog
ELVIRA	Unsuccessful samor in Mozart's *Don Giovanni*
ELVIS	Nothin' but a hound dog

ELWOOD	Tall and gawky
E MAIL	You found it through the bulletin board
EMAR	For a red classic tabby Cymric Manx . . . they are intelligent with a rabbitlike posture.
EMBER	For a black cat . . . or a red cat
EMELLE	For a blue-cream and white Scottish fold . . . they are placid and have the cutest ears.
EMERALD	For a jewel of a pet
EMERSON	For a radio buff
EMERY	For someone who gets board easily (I hope you get that)
EMILE	For a pet from the South Pacific
EMILIO	For a pet with a lot of brothers
EMILY	For a Dickinson fan
EMIR	For an Oriental shorthair
EMMA	For a brindle Great Dane
EMMANUELLE	For an X-rated pet
EMMAUS	Pet birds
EMMERY	Has a purring quality . . . for contented cats
EMMETT	A clown's pet
EMMY	A soap star's pet
EMPEROR	For a well dressed pet
EMPIRE	A very large or very high waisted pet, or a pet that strikes back
EMPRESS	You named your first pet Princess, but now you've grown.
EMU	Bird that's lost the art of flying
ENAMEL	Pet turtles

ENCHILADA	Chihuahua, Mexican hairless
ENCODER	A pet with a spotted coat
ENCORE	For a brood mare
ENCYCLOPEDIA	For a bloodhound
ENERGY	Any of the terriers
ENGARDE	Attack or guard dogs
ENGINEER	Bees, ants, pets that do things you don't quite understand
ENGLEBERT	Best when paired with a Humperdinck
ENGLISH	Yorkshire terrier, Norwich terrier, King Charles spaniel, etcetera
ENGLISH CHANNEL	Your fish tank
ENGLISH MUFFIN	For an English bulldog . . . can you just see it?
ENNUI	For a lethargic pet
ENOCH	For the pet you thought had disappeared
ENOIVE	Rabbits, hamsters, gerbils
ENOUGH	For the runt of the last litter
ENQUIRER	A gossip's pet or for those with inquiring minds
ENRIGHT	"McMillan and Wife," a police dog
ENVELOPE	For pet turtles
ENZO	For somone who would like to own an Italian restaurant
ENZYME	Pets with delicate stomachs
EOS	Early risers
EPHROM	Male and funny
EPHRON	Female and funny
EPIC	A large, heroic pet

EPICENTER	A pet that demands a lot of attention
EPICURUS	Loves you for pleasure
EPILOGUE	The last of the litter
EPITOME	A pet you plan to show and win with
EPONINE	For a *Les Mis* fan
EPOXY	For a fiercely loyal pet
EQUALIZER	Dobermans, Alsatians, rottweilers, etcetera
EQUINOX	For a day and night dog
EQUUS	Pet horse
ERATO	For a basenji
ERDMAN	Sounds a little like ''nerdman,'' so for a funny-looking pet that seems to need glasses.
EREBUS	Pets with dark coats
ERGO	Any offspring of your male and female pets
ERIC	Red Abyssinian, red Devon rex, red Irish setter, or Norwegian elkhound
ERICA	Pets with a fear of flying
ERIN	An Irish pet
ERMA	For a deuce of any kind
ERNEST	Outdoor, macho, Hemingwayesque
ERNESTO	Spanish, outdoor, macho, Hemingwayesque
ERNIE	''My Three Sons'' ... one of your three pets, or pair with Bert if you only have two
ERNST	Perfect for a bullfrog
EROS	Lovebirds
ERRATA	You regret this one, or a pet that refuses to house train

ERROL	Dark, adventurous, leading man type
ERSATZ	For mixed breeds
ERTÉ	An artist's pet
ERWIN	An American foxhound, beagle, Cairn terrier, cocker spaniel, or dachshund
ERWITT	A photogenic dog (photographer Eliot Erwitt)
ESCROW	The pet you've bought for protection
ESDRAS	Four books of the Old Testament
ESKIMO	Alaskan malamutes, Eskimo dogs
ESMERALDA	Wonderful cat or reptile name
ESP	The dog that brings coffee with your morning paper
ESPADRILLE	A summer pet
ESPRESSO	Brown Burmese, Havana brown, Irish water spaniel, etcetera
ESQUIRE	Wears a monocle
ESSAY	A pet that makes a statement
ESSIE	Soft-coated wheaten terrier . . . originally from Ireland . . . courageous and active
ESTEE	A pet with eyeliner markings
ESTELLE	A throwback to the fifties
ESTHER	A throwback to the Bible
E. T.	A pug, or any animal that calls home often
ETCETERA	Insect collections, or a mutt
ETCH-A-SKETCH	Cats that claw the furniture
ETHAN	Partial to antique furniture
ETHAN ALLEN	Partial to antique furniture reproductions
ETHEL	Lucy's friend and neighbor

ETHER	For sleepy pets
ETHYL	For a pet into alcohol
ETON	English bulldogs, English spaniels, et-cetera, or for a private school person
ETOS	For a greyhound . . . intelligent but often undervalued because of its re-served behavior
ETTA	Pair her with Quette
ET TU?	For a pet you shouldn't trust
EUCLID	Pets with geometric markings
EUGENE	For an O'Neill fan
EUNICE	Funny-looking female
EUPHORIA	An uncaged bird
EUREKA	The pet that replaces your vacuum when it comes to cleaning up the kitchen floor
EUROPA	Bulldog
EUSTACE	Funny-looking male
EVAN	I like it for a collie. After all, they can't all be Lassie. But it's hard to find one that fits.
EVANS	Rogers' mate
EVE	First born
EVELYN	Usually your best friend's mother
EVENING SHADE	Deep gray or blue to black coloring
EVEREST	A very tall example of its species
EVERETT	For a pet that doesn't like to be cooped up (C. Everett)
EVERGLADE	A pet from Florida
EVERGREEN	Turtles and frogs that live to a ripe old age

EVERT	Baseline fish with two-handed backstroke
EVIAN	Fresh fish, or a pet that only drinks from the toilet bowl
EVITA	Strong female songbirds
EWING	Great Danes, Irish wolfhounds, borzois, Scottish deerhounds
EX	Reminds you of ...
EXAMINER	Particularly curious cats
EXCALIBUR	Snakes
EXCAVATOR	Dig, dig, dig
EXCESS	Breeding rabbits
EXEC	Trained to carry a briefcase
EXIT	Manx, Japanese bobtail, malamute, Siberian husky ... anything with a stumped tail
EXPECTER	Waits to greet your guests
EXPLORER	Pets that periodically disappear
EXPORT	French poodles, English spaniels, Japanese bobtails, etcetera
EXPRESS	Greyhounds
EXPRESSO	Hyper Italian greyhounds
EXPRESSWAY	For a pet that can't relax and is always running, or bossy greyhounds
EYEFUL	For a pug, King Charles spaniel, cocker spaniel, anything with big eyes
EYEWITNESS	Seeing-Eye dogs
EZEKIEL	A prophetic animal
EZRA	For a pharaoh hound ... ancient Egyptian dog brought to Spain ... docile, loyal, and playful
EZRA POUND	You got him from the ASPCA

F. SCOTT	What a fabulous name for a pet
F. M.	A DJ's pet
FABERGÉ	For any pet that can lay an egg
FABIAN	For a songbird, with an occasional foray into movies
FABRIZIO	An Italian hound ... strong and muscular, vivacious, a hunter
FACE	For that absolutely gorgeous pet, or someone that was into "The A Team"
FACT FINDER	An insurance adjuster's pet
FADDIS	A Westphalian basset ... combative, intelligent, and friendly
FADIMA	A blue Tonkinese
FAGIN	For a shady character
FAHRENHEIT	Centigrade's companion
FAIRBANKS	An Alaskan malamute
FAIRCHILD	For an English springer spaniel
FAIRFAX	An apartment building in New York City that used to be the FBI building
FAIR LADY	For a feminine feline

FAISAL	A king . . . a King Charles spaniel is of mixed ancestry, so it might work . . . good for any strong-willed pet
FAITH	For someone who believes they've found a swan
FAITHFUL	For the swan you've found. They mate for life.
FALA	For a Christmas pet . . . la la la
FALCHI	For someone who likes handbags
FALCON	A parakeet
FALINE	A character from *Bambi*
FALKLAND	For a pet from an island
FAMOUS AMOS	For a chocolate-colored pet
FANDANGO	Trip the light fandango. Are those the right words to the song?
FANG	Great for a dog with a bad temper
FANISHIA	For a blue Abyssinian
FANNIE	For a pet with a broad backside
FANNY FARMER	For a Belgian sheepdog, or for someone who got his or her broad backside from chocolates
FANTASIA	When you can't believe that you've given in and actually gotten a pet
FANTASTIC	When Fantasia has worked out and you get a second one
FANTOM	What you wish Fantasia was if it doesn't work out
FANTUM	For a silky terrier
FANZINE	A pet that's a fan of housebreaking on magazines rather than newspapers
FARCUS	For a German wirehaired pointer
FARFEL	A good name for male pets

FARKAS	For a Welsh corgi
FARLEY	For a shorthaired Saint Bernard
FARMER BROTHER	For a border collie
FARNSWORTH	A character in *Heaven Can Wait*
FARNUM	For an Old English sheepdog
FAROUK	Another king . . . King Charles spaniel name
FARRAH	For an Afghan . . . great hair
FARRER	For a smooth fox terrier
FARRIS	For a Westphalian basset
FAST FORWARD	Another one for the hyperactive type
FAT CAT	Just that
FATAL ATTRACTION	For a pet that you can't resist who will eventually be your undoing
FATHER MULCAHY	Another of the ''M*A*S*H'' characters
FATIMA	For an Egyptian mau
FAULKNER	For an English bulldog
FAUST	For an English foxhound
FAUZI	A pharaoh hound
FAWN	For a fawn Abyssinian
FAX	For a very busy pet
FAY	For a nonpedigree longhair
FAY WRAY	For anyone associated with a gorilla
FEARLESS	For any gorilla associated with Fay Wray
FEATHERS	For a bird
FEATHER-WEIGHT	For a light pet

FEBRUARY	For a pet born in February
FEDERICO	For a Fellini fan
FEEDBACK	For a parrot
FEE FEE	For a French bulldog
FEENEY	Shirley
FEETS	For a pet with multicolored paws able to leap tall buildings in a single bound
FEIFFER	Jules
FELDER	A divorced person's pet
FELICE	Happy, in Italian
FELICIA	For a happy tortie and white Scottish fold
FELICIANO	For a pet into lighting fires
FELICITY	For a very happy pet
FELIX	The cat, the wonderful, wonderful cat, or Oscar's roommate
FELLA	For a "most happy"
FELLER	For a male Labrador retriever
FELLINI	For an Italian pointer . . . thoughtful, docile, loyal, not excessively cheerful
FEMME FATALE	For a golden Persian
FENDI	A pet into labels
FENWAY	A baseball stadium. For a pet with Red Sox, perhaps?
FERGIE	For a red royal standard
FERGUS	For a golden retriever
FERGUSON	Another wonderful pet name
FERNANDO	A cat that likes to "hide away"
FERRAGAMO	For an Italian pointer

FERRARI	For an Italian greyhound . . . speed
FERRIS	For a gerbil . . . round and round and round and round
FESTER	I would use this for a slightly distasteful pet . . . snakes, for instance
FETA	For a Greek hound
FETCHIT	For a real comedian
FIAT	For a cream shaded cameo tabby European shorthair
FIBBER MCGEE	And Molly
FIDDLER	A roofer's pet
FIDDLEDEE DEE	For a *Gone With the Wind* fan
FIDEL	For a Cuban pet
FIDO	Well, finally, a name that's really a name!
FIELDER	A pet that likes to chase balls
FIELD MARSHAL	For a Deutsche dogge
FIEVEL	For a pet going west
FIGARO	An opera lover's pet
FIJI	For a pet from the Pacific Islands
FILBERT	For a nut
FILENE	For a pet that has to live in the basement
FILIBUSTER	For a parrot
FILLIPA	For a Swedish shepherd . . . courageous and independent
FILOFAX	A very organized person's pet
FINANCE	An accountant's pet
FINCHLEY	For a Great Pyrenees . . . very big, hardworking, affectionate

FINDLAY	A gallery
FINDLEY	A mere name
FINGERPRINT	For a policeman's dog
FINKE	For a Finnish hound
FINOLA	For a Finnish spitz
FIONA	Any English pet with a bent toward snobbish behavior
FIORELLO	For someone who flys to LaGuardia a lot
FIRE EATER	For a pit bull
FIREWATER	For a cat that keeps trying to get into the fish tank
FIREWORKS	For the cat that succeeds in getting into the fish tank
FIROOZ	For an Egyptian mau
FIRST LADY	For a household full of boys
FISH	For a Portuguese water dog
FITCHLY	A town in England
FITZGERALD	An Irish water spaniel
FITZI	Fitzpatrick's nickname
FITZPATRICK	Fitzi's full name
FLACK	For a pet that talks back, or a Roberta fan
FLAME	For a red Abyssinian
FLAN	A dessert eater's pet
FLAPJACK	A pancake lover's pet
FLASH	For a very fast pet
FLASH DANCE	For any fast dancing pet
FLASH GORDON	Those were the days

FLATFOOT	Another policeman's pet (see Fingerprint)
FLAUBERT	French novelist . . . *Madame Bovary*
FLEETWOOD	A chauffeur's pet
FLEISCHMANN	I can't believe it's not pedigree
FLETCH	A bumbling detective's pet
FLETCHER	A detective writer's pet
FLINTSTONE	If you really love it, go for it
FLIP	For a pet that can do somersaults
FLIPPER	A dolphin or other fish
FLOPPER	For an uncoordinated pet
FLORA	A green pet
FLORENCE	A city in Italy
FLORIDA	A sun lover's pet
FLORIE	For a Siamese
FLORIS	For a shorthaired Scottish fold
FLOSSIE	A dentist's pet
FLOSSY	A dentist's pet
FLOUR	A cook's pet
FLOWER	A gardener's pet
FLOYD	A boxer's pet
FODOR	For a guide dog
FODORA	For a Himalayan
FOGEL	For an Irish wolfhound
FOGGY	For a pet with a poor sense of direction
FOLDER	For someone from Manila
FOLLY	For a Skye terrier
FONDUE	For *un chien français*
FONTEYN	For a white West Highland terrier

FOO FOO	For a Samoyed . . . they just look foo foo, all puffy, fluffy, and white
FOOSHA	For an Oriental shorthair
FOOTPRINT	For a Newfoundland. Now that's a footprint.
FORBES	For an intelligent pet
FORD	A pet for a Harrison
FOREMAN	For a Staffordshire bull terrier . . . combative but steady
FOREPLAY	For a dog that likes to tease before biting
FORESIGHT	A dog that doesn't use foreplay
FOREST	For a Black Forest hound . . . the Czechoslovakian national hound . . . independent and a good sense of direction
FORMAGGIO	An Italian animal partial to hard, grating cheeses
FORSYTH	For a pet that has foresight but also a lisp
FORT APACHE	For someone from the Bronx
FORTESQUE	Although a great name for any male, I like it for the Scottish terrier
FORTUNE	For any pet that cost more than five hundred dollars
FOSDICK	For a Maine coon
FOSSE	A dancer's pet
FOSTER	For a whippet
FOTO	A photographer's pet
FOUAD	For a pharaoh hound . . . loyal and very playful
FOULARD	A tie maven's pet

FOUNTAIN-BLEAU	For someone who used to travel to Miami in the sixties
FOURTH OF JULY	A pet born on Independence Day
FOUZI	For an Egyptian mau
FOXIE	An American fox terrier
FRACK	*See* Frick
FRANCESCA	A female Spanish greyhound . . . aristocratic and courageous
FRANCIS	An Anglo-Spanish greyhound
FRANCISCO	A male Spanish greyhound
FRANCO	For a dictatorial Spanish mastiff
FRANK	An American fox hound
FRANKFURTER	I'm sorry, but a judgmental dachshund it must be
FRANKIE	His nickname
FRANKLIN	For a Ben or pair with Eleanor
FRANKO	For a spinone Italiano . . . although they are gentle and good-natured
FRANZ	For someone who is on the list
FRANZETTI	For a spinone Italiano . . . solid, sturdy hunting dog. Sociable, affectionate, and adaptable
FRASIER	An acting psychiatrist's pet
FRAÜLEIN	For a German shepherd
FRAU ZEITZ	My German teacher
FRAZER	For a wirehaired dachshund with glasses
FRECKLES	A dalmatian
FRED	For a silky terrier
FREDDIE	An Australian terrier
FREDDY	An Australian silky terrier

FREDERIC	For a miniature schnauzer
FREDERICK	For someone who dresses from Hollywood
FREEDOM	For a border collie or a Bosnian hound
FREELANCE	For a pet that has more than one owner
FREEWAY	The dog from the series "Hart to Hart"
FRENCH FRY	For a French spaniel
FRENCH TOAST	For a French pointer
FRESH	For a "cool" pet
FRET	A guitarist's pet
FREUD	For someone in analysis for years and years
FRIAR TUCK	For someone who lives in a forest
FRICK	A museum in New York
FRICK	*See* Frack
FRIDAY	My gal
FRIEDA	For an American shorthair
FRIEND HARE	A character from *Bambi*
FRISBEE	For a dog you have to catch
FRISKIE	Definitely for one of the terriers
FRISKY	For a wirehaired terrier
FRITZ	For a male schnauzer
FRITZI	For a female schnauzer
FRIZZY	For a puli ... they have those long, curly locks that reach the ground
FROMAGE	A French animal partial to soft, runny cheeses
FROMM	An analyst's pet

FROSTIE	For a Siberian husky
FROSTING	For a pet that's not satisfied with its hair color
FROSTY	For an Iceland dog
FRUMPSON	For the son of a frump
FUDGE	A chocoholic's pet
FUGITIVE	For a dog that keeps running away
FULLER BRUSH	For a pet that goes from house to house
FU MANCHU	For any of your Chinese breeds . . . Lhasa apsos, Shih Tzus, chow chows, Shar-peis etcetera
FUNK	For a depressed pet
FUNKY	For a happy pet
FUNNY FACE	For Fred Astaire and Audrey Hepburn fans
FURROUK	For a furry king
FUSCHIA	For a colorful pet
FUSILLI	Another one for pulis . . . long, curly hair
FUTURE SHOCK	For a pet that will grow far bigger than you anticipated
FUZZY	For a pet with memory loss
FUZZY WUZZY	What they said about Fuzzy

G. I. JOE	Definitely for a boxer, bulldog, or wirehaired dachshund
GABBY	One of those adorable names that would be good for any cute animal, or a talking parrot
GABBY HAYES	Roy Rogers' sidekick
GABE	Always reminds me of ''Welcome Back, Kotter''
GABLE	For a Clark fan
GABOR	For a femme fatale
GABRIEL	For a pet that blows his horn
GABRIELLE	For a more formal cute animal
GAEL	For a frog or a turtle
GAIETY	For an absolutely, positively, constantly happy pet
GAINESFORT	For a slower moving animal, like an English mastiff
GAINS-BOROUGH	For a pet that knows good art when it sees it
GALATEA	Very regal . . . for a pet with extreme poise and great posture
GALAXY	For a pet that's got its head in the clouds

GALBRAITH	For an economical pet
GAL FRIDAY	For a pet you bring to the office with you
GALILEO	For a stargazer
GALLANT	For a polite pet
GALLOP	For a horse that likes to run
GALLUP	For a horse that likes to jump polls
GAMBLER	For a pet that does tightrope tricks, or travels to Vegas a lot
GAMEBOY	For a pet whose home is addicted to the game
GANNETT	For a pet that only uses local papers
GARBO	For a cat that "vants to be alone"
GARCIA	For a Spanish mastiff
GARÇON	A waiter's pet
GARDENER	For the pet that constantly digs up the yard
GARDENIA	For a white Persian, or a Vincent
GARFIELD	Yeah, yeah, it's already been done. And, if you do it, people will marvel at your lack of originality.
GARFUNKEL	For a songbird
GARIBALDI	Italian patriot
GARLAND	Judy, Judy, Judy
GARLIC	For a pet with bad breath
GARLIK	For a pet that buys the pills instead
GARNET	For any red pet
GARP	For a pet that thinks the world goes according to it
GARRISON	For a pet from Lake Wobegon
GARROWAY	For a faithful "Today Show" fan

GARTH	For a pet that will live on a brook
GARVEY	For a baseball fan
GARY	A pet from Indiana
GAS MAN	A Con Ed man's pet
GATEWAY	A bridge inspector's pet
GATSBY	For a rich, loose pet
GATWAY	For a blue-cream smoke Cornish rex
GATWICK	For a pet that likes to go to England
GAUDÍ	For a very ostentatious pet
GAUGUIN	Artist
GAZA	For a patrol dog
GAZA STRIPPER	For a cane nudo (no hair, just a tuft on its head)
GAZELLE	For a greyhound, nice and fast
GAZPACHO	For a real mix
GEDRICK	Sounds like a hairstylist
GEISHA	For a Japanese bobtail or Japanese spitz
GEM	For a pearl of a pet
GEMINI	For a pet born from May twenty-second to June twenty-first
GEMMA	A gemologist's pet
GENERAL	For a boxer, bulldog, or other authoritative type
GENESIS	A teenager's pet
GENEVA	For a Swiss hound
GENIUS	Either a very smart or a very dumb pet
GENOVA	For an Italian pointer, Italian greyhound, etcetera
GENTLE BEN	CBS TV show, 1967–1969

GEORGE	Boy
GEORGETOWN	A politician's pet
GEORGETTE	Ted's wife on ''The Mary Tyler Moore Show''
GEORGIA	For the pet that stays on your mind
GEORGIA BROWN	For a sweet pet
GEORGINA	For a feisty Georgia
GERALD	For a not-so-suave American bluetick coonhound
GERALDINE	For a female, not-so-suave American bluetick coonhound
GERALDO	For a feisty pet
GERANIUM	For a pet with a big, sweet face
GERARD	For an English mastiff
GERARDO	For a Spanish mastiff
GERBER	For a pet with a baby face
GERBER BABY	For a dog that is only going to be fed baby food
GERMAINE	For a pet that makes a difference
GERONIMO	For a pet that has no boundaries
GERRI	For a German spaniel
GERSHWIN	For a cat that likes to walk the piano keys
GERT	For
GERTIE	a
GERTRUDE	cat
GESTALT	For a pet that gets the whole picture
GET SMART	For a Maxwell

GETTYSBURG	For a pet that always knows its address
GHIDRAH	The three-headed monster
GHOST	For an all-white pet, or Mrs. Muir
GHOSTBUSTER	For a bigger and meaner pet than Ghost
GIACOMETTI	Artist
GIANNI	For a small continental spaniel
GIBSON	For a Bedlington terrier
GIBSON GIRL	Fat chance
GIDEON	For a pet with a horn
GIDGET	Sandra Dee ... the Big Cahuna ... those were the days
GIFFORD	For a pet that likes to follow football ... Frank paired with Kathie Lee
GIGI	For a French bulldog
GILBERT	For a chow chow
GILBERT GRAPE	For a chow chow that likes grapes
GILDA	For a wonderful, funny pet
GILES	For a butler
GILL	For a fish
GILLESPIE	For a dizzy pet
GILLI	For a Bedlington terrier. Looks like a sheep and likes to catch rats
GILLIGAN	For a pet you'd like to send to an island
GILLIS	Dobie ... from the TV show of the early 1960's
GILLYFLOWER	Such a cute name ... a wiggly, happy Cairn terrier

GILMORE	For a cocker spaniel or a chocolate tortie Burmese
GILROY	For a Cairn terrier ... lively, cheerful, and lovable ... Toto from *The Wizard of Oz*
GIMBEL'S	Where Macy's will possibly follow
GIMLET	For a Saint Bernard
GINGER	There are an amazing number of dogs named Ginger
GINGERBREAD	An alternative to Ginger
GINGER ROGERS	And Fred Astaire
GINO	For a Bolognese
GIORDANO	For an Italian greyhound
GIORGIO	For a pet from Beverly Hills. Perfect for a very suave Spinone Italiano (dog)
GIOVANNA	For a female pet recently over from Italy
GIOVANNI	For a male pet recently over from Italy
GIRL SCOUT	For a real goody two shoes
GISH	Lillian and Dorothy
GIVENCHY	For a very fancy, well dressed pet
GIZMO	An inventor's pet
GLADIOLA	For a very feminine, flowery pet
GLADYS	For a bulldog
GLAMOUR PUSS	That is so cute
GLEE	For a particularly happy pet
GLEN	For an outdoor pet
GLENDA	For a tall, dark, and female outdoor pet

GLENLIVET	A drinker's pet
GLICK	For one of the smaller animals, like a hamster, turtle, fish, etcetera
GLORIA	For a calico American wirehair
GLORY	For a red, white, and blue American shorthair
GLOVER	For a baseball catcher
GNASHER	Pair with Wolf from *Wuthering Heights,* or a pet with huge teeth
GNOCCHI	For a potato fan
GOALIE	For a Jack Russell terrier . . . they keep going after that ball
GOBLET	For a very fancy pet that eats from a silver bowl and drinks from a goblet
GOBO	A character from *Bambi*
GODDARD	For someone who likes to clean silver
GODFATHER	For a rottweiler
GODFREY	For a serious pet
GODFRIED	An English foxhound
GODIVA	Another good name for an Afghan
GODZILLA	For a very menacing pet
GOITER	Ooh, I don't like it
GOLD RUSH	For a golden retriever who likes to play fetch
GOLDA	For a strong, female golden retriever
GOLD DIGGER	For a weak male golden retriever
GOLDEN BOY	golden retriever
GOLDEN GIRL	golden retriever
GOLDFINGER	golden retriever
GOLDIE	golden retriever
GOLDILOCKS	golden retriever or a puli

GOLDWATER	A Republican golden retriever, or one that's not quite housebroken
GOLIATH	An Irish wolfhound, borzoi, deerhound . . . any pet that can put its paws on your shoulders when it jumps up to greet you
GOMER	For a pet that leaves a pile
GOMEZ	For a suave character
GONZALEZ	For a Mexican hairless dog
GONZO	For a "Muppets" fan, or any pet that's slightly nutty
GOOBER	For a movie goer. Pair with Raisinette
GOOD AND PLENTY	For a dalmatian, or for a good, big animal, like a Saint Bernard
GOODSPEED	For a fast pet
GOODWILL	For a pet from the ASPCA
GOOFY	Disney's "goofy" dog
GOOSEBERRY	For a small pet
GOOSEBUMP	For an even smaller pet
GOPHER	For a "Love Boat" fan
GORBACHEV	For a formal Russian wolfhound
GORBIE	For an informal Russian wolfhound
GORDIMER	For an English-German mix
GORDON	A gin lover's pet
GORDY	*Stand By Me*
GORGEOUS GEORGE	George Wagner, the wrestler . . . good for a blond pet
GORKY	For a pet that likes to go to the park
GOSSETT	For a tall, lean, muscular pet with fierce eyes
GOTFRIED	For a German shepherd

GOTHAM	Another choice for a silver cleaning fanatic
GOUDA	Contains more fat than Edam
GOURMET	For a pet that won't touch dry food
GOVERNOR	For a pet that will become president
GOYA	For a pet that's full of beans
GRABLE	A dog with good legs
GRACE	For a religious pet
GRACIE	For a George Burns and Gracie Allen fan
GRACIELLA	For an Italian pointer . . . although they tend not to be too cheerful
GRADUATE	For a pet that will have to go through obedience training more than once
GRADY	For a scruffy pet
GRAF	A tennis aficionado's pet
GRAFITTI	For a pet that likes to mark his territory
GRAHAM	For a cracker or a parrot
GRAINGER	For an American foxhound
GRANDE DAME	Wonderful for a female Saint Bernard, borzoi, Newfoundland, etcetera
GRANDMA MOSES	Artist. For an old-looking pet
GRAND MARNIER	An after dinner pet
GRAND PRIX	A race car driver's pet
GRAND SLAM	A tennis player's pet
GRANGER	I like this name. It's strong and seems excellent for a confident pet.
GRANITE	For a pet that's hard to move . . . or shall we say obstinate

GRANNIE	For an old, fat cat
GRANOLA	For a lumpy cat
GRANT	Another Union pet. Pair with Lee
GRAPHIC	A pet that uses its paws when communicating
GRAVLAX	Fish
GRAY	For a silver tabby Persian (it looks gray)
GRAZIE	For a very thankful person
GRAZIELLA	For a Maltese
GREAT GATSBY	For a harlequin Great Dane
GRECO	For a Spanish water dog
GREELEY	Horace
GREEN BERET	For a bulldog, boxer, rottweiler, or pit bull ... good in the protection area
GREENSTREET	Sydney ... good for a fat pet
GREENWICH	For a pet from Connecticut or the Village
GREER	A pet for a feminist
GREGORY	For a woodpecker
GREMLIN	For a pug or a King Charles spaniel
GRETA	For someone who likes Garbo
GRETCHEN	For a cute female schnauzer
GRETEL	Hansel's pair
GREY	For a silver spotted British shorthair (it looks grey)
GREYSTOKE	For a monkey
GRIFFEN	For a parakeet
GRIFFIN	Pair with Sabine ... lovebirds
GRIMALDI	For a pet from Monaco
GRIMES	For a Tennessee treeing brindle

GRIMM	For someone into fairy tales
GRISELDA	Great cat name
GRISWALD	A Royal Standard poodle
GRODY	A tough little Scottish terrier
GROMYKO	For a Russian wolfhound
GROUCHO	Either for a Marx fan, or for a grouch
GROVER	For a blue pet that's always sniffing in the garbage can
GSTAAD	A skier's pet
G-STRING	For a French poodle
GUARDIAN	For a rottweiler
GUBER	A producer's pet
GUCCI	*See* ''Triples,'' Fendi and Mark Cross
GUESS	For a pet of mixed parentage
GUGGENHEIM	For a pet that appreciates fine art
GUILLERMO	A Spanish William, possibly for a Chihuahua?
GUINEVERE	That naughty queen from Camelot
GUINNESS	For an Alec, or a beer lover
GULLIVER	For a pet that likes to travel
GUMBEL	For an early morning pet
GUMBO	For a pet that likes soup
GUMP	For an incredibly lucky, very limited pet
GUNNAR	For a German shorthaired pointer
GUNS	Roses' mate
GUNSMOKE	For anyone who watched TV in the sixties
GUS	For a basset hound
GUSSIE	For an American pet
GUSTAF	For a French pet

GUSTAV	For a German pet
GUSTAVO	For a Spanish pet
GUSTO	For a pet with a flair for eating big and quick
GUSTOFF	For a Swiss pet
GUTHRIE	For an Arlo
GUY	*See* "Doubles," Guy and Gal
GWEN	For a cream lynx point shorthair
GWENDOLYN	For a cream silver Somali
GWYNNE	For a Cockatiel
GYPSY	For a multicolored orange, white, and black cat
GYPSY ROSE	*See* Gaza Stripper

H. STERN	For a jewel of a pet, with franchises all over the world
HACKETT	For your buddy
HADDIE	For a Black Forest hound
HAFIZ	A musician's pet
HAILEY	For a brown California spangled longhair
HAKIM	For someone into Arabic names . . . this one means doctor
HALEVI	For a Yugoslavian tricolor hound
HALFBACK	Cute for a big animal
HALF PINT	Cute for a small animal
HALIFAX	For a cold animal
HALIMA	For a tortie smoke European shorthair
HALLE	For a Dutch sheepdog
HALLEY	The comet . . . for a pet you expect to live till the age of seventy-six
HALLIE	For a brown mackerel tabby American wirehair
HALSEY	For a lavender classic tabby
HALSTON	A designer's pet

HAMILL	A skater's pet
HAMILTON	A politician's pet
HAMISH	For a very affectionate lap dog
HAMLET	An English major's pet
HAMLISCH	A name for someone who enjoys Marvin
HAMMACHER	A shopper's pet
HAMMERSTEIN	Oscar's partner
HAMPDEN	For an American foxhound
HAMPTON	For a pet that likes Long Island
HANCOCK	For a pet with a good signature
HANDEL	Composer
HANDLEY	For a monkey
HANDSOME DEVIL	The Yale mascot (white bulldog)
HANDY	For a pet that can fix things
HANGER	A pilot's pet
HANINA	For an Egyptian mau
HANK	For a tough-guy pet
HANKS	For a tomcat
HANNAH	For a soft, motherly cat
HANNIBAL	For a great warrior
HANS	For a Christian Andersen
HANTUSHA	My Lhasa Apso's (Tusha) Formal name . . . it means sweetheart in Arabic
HAPPINESS	For a pet with a perpetual smile on its face
HAPPY	For someone with a lot of money
HAPPY TRAILS	''The Roy Rogers Show''

HARBOR MASTER	For any of the water spaniels
HARDING	A pet with a severe jealous streak
HARD ROCK	For someone who enjoys going to cafés
HARDWICKE	For a pit bull
HARDY	See ''Doubles,'' Laurel and Hardy
HARKNESS	For a pet with large ears and great hearing
HARLEAN	For a harlequin Great Dane
HARLEY	A motorcycle person's pet
HARLOT	Well, I don't think so
HARLOW	For a sexy pet
HARMONY	For a pet that receives strangers well
HAROLD	Perfect for a hamster
HARPER	For a bazaar pet
HARPIGNIES	Artist's pet
HARPO	For a pet that doesn't talk
HARRIMAN	For a very distinguished, diplomatic pet
HARRINGTON	For an Irish setter
HARRIS	For a pollster
HARRISON	For a person who drives a Ford
HARRY	For a dirty dog (two puns in one!)
HARRY WINSTON	For a pet that knows the finer things in life
HART	Hartley's nickname
HARTLEY	For a pet that would wear tassel loafers if it could
HARVARD	An Ivy Leaguer's pet
HARVEST	For a pet from the Midwest

HARVEY	For a rabbit
HARVEY WALLBANGER	For a rabbit that drinks too much
HASKELL	Pal Eddie on "Leave It to Beaver"
HASLETT	Doctor in "Murder, She Wrote"
HASSAN	For a horse
HASSELHOFF	For any of the water spaniels
HASTY	For a pet you chose incorrectly
HASTY PUDDING	For a Yorkshire terrier you chose incorrectly
HATTIE	For a collie
HAVI	For the separated part of a Siamese
HAVOC	For the pet that takes over the house
HAWK	For a Doberman
HAWKEYE	For a bird dog
HAWKINS	A pet for a Sadie
HAWORTH	For a bluetick coonhound
HAYAKAWA	For a Pekingese, or a dog that sleeps all the time
HAYDN	Composer's pet
HAYWORTH	The Rita for whom I was named. Can you imagine?
HAZE	For a pet that strolls around in a fog
HAZEL	The name my parents tried to call me before my uncle intervened. Can you imagine?
HEALER	A doctor's pet
HEARST	A magazine reader's pet
HEART	For a pet near and dear
HEATH BAR	For a chocolate and toffee colored animal

HEATHCLIFF	A dark, brooding, and romantic English pet
HEATHCOTE	For an Old English mastiff
HEATHER	A quiet, gentle pet
HEATHROW	A stewardess' pet
HECTOR	For a Spanish greyhound
HECTOR GARCIA	Who *is* Hector Garcia?
HEFNER	For the head bunny
HEIDI	For a Swiss hound
HEIFETZ	A musician's pet
HEINZ	For a pet with fifty-seven different personalities
HELMSLEY	For a pet with tax problems
HELMUT	Great for a doberman
HELOISE	For a pet that likes to give hints
HEMINGWAY	For an ernest pet
HENDERSON	A pet for a Florence
HENDRIX	A pet for a Jimmy
HENLEY	For a Gordon setter
HENNY YOUNGMAN	A comedian's pet
HENRI	For a Bendel's shopper
HENRIETTA	For a female Bendel's shopper
HENRIK	For a German Bendel's shopper
HENRY	For an American Bendel's shopper
HENRY BROWN	A farmer's pet
HEPBURN	For anyone who watches *Breakfast at Tiffany's* more than once a year
HEPWORTH	For a Clumber spaniel
HER	*See* "Doubles," Him and Her

HERA	Zeus' sister
HERBERT	One of the greats. This name is appropriate for any pet.
HERBIE	A Scottish terrier
HERCEMER	For a red Abyssinian
HERCULE	For a Poirot fan
HERCULES	Either a Yorkie or a rottweiler
HERE'S JOHNNY	A late night pet
HERMALENE	For a Rhodesian ridgeback
HERMAN	A hermit crab
HERMÈS	For a pet that wears a scarf
HERMINIE	Wonderful for a big, fat, furry car
HERMITAGE	For a Russian pet, or you loved the museum
HERO	For a Saint Bernard, or a pet that likes big sandwiches
HERRINGBONE	For a cross between a dog and a cat . . . herring for the cat and bone for the dog
HERSCHEL	What a Basset hound
HERSHEL	For a silver spotted British shorthair
HERSHEY	For a chocolate-loving dog
HERTZ	For a pet that likes to rent cars
HESPERUS	Evening star
HESTER	For a longhaired calico or one that wears a scarlet letter A
HEYWARD	For a person who calls Ward often
HEYWOOD	For a person who calls Wood often
HIALIAH	Perfect for a greyhound
HIAM	La . . . for a healthy pet

HICCUP	Nice one for a Saint Bernard
HICKORY	For a flavorful pet
HIGGINS	For an Irish water spaniel
HIGH ANXIETY	Mel Brooks
HIGH CLASS	Grace Kelly
HIGH ENERGY	Jerry Lewis
HIGHNESS	An Irish wolfhound
HIGH SOCIETY	Bing Crosby
HILDA	For a German shepherd
HILDEGARDE	Her sister
HILTON	For a pet that travels well
HIM	*See* "Doubles," Him and Her
HINDRANCE	For a pet that doesn't travel well
HINLEY	For a red Oriental shorthair
HIPPOCRATES	For a healthy pet
HIRSCHL	A cream tabby point Devon rex
HITCHCOCK	For a mystery fan
HOAGY	For a dachshund
HOBART	For a Great Pyrenees
HOBSON	For an Irish setter
HOCKNEY	For a pet that's into swimming pools
HODGE	*See* "Doubles," Hodge and Podge
HODGES	For a pet that serves you
HOFFA	For a pet that's neither here nor there
HOGAN	A scrappy, wiry mutt
HOGAN'S HERO	For the owner of the scrappy, wiry mutt
HOKUSAI	For a Japanese bobtail
HOLDEN	A pet for a William
HOLIDAY	For a pet you bought on vacation

HOLLING	For a "Northern Exposure" fan
HOLLY	A hunter's pet
HOLLYWOOD	For a real show dog
HOLMES	A detective's pet
HOME BOY	For one of the cats in the 'hood
HOMER	For a dog that's into "The Simpsons"
HONEY	A favorite for golden retrievers
HONEY BUN	Any golden-color pet
HONEYCHAR	Another for the goldens
HONEYMIST	A golden Persian
HONEYSUCKLE	For a rose
HONG-CHOO	For a Chinese temple dog
HOODLUM	For one of those dogs that has circles around its eyes
HOOLIGAN	For an Irish racoon or any pet that's ill behaved
HOOVER	For a pet that eats absolutely everything in sight
HOPKINS	For an English springer spaniel
HOPSACK	For an akita
HORACE	When was the last time you met a Horace?
HORATIO	For a giant schnauzer
HORNE	For a pet that lets you lean (Lena) on it
HOROSCOPE	An astrologer's pet
HORTENSE	An elephant
HORTON	An elephant too
HOSMER	A Swedish shepherd
HOSS	Brother to Little Joe and Adam

HOT DIGGIDY, DOG DIGGIDY	A dachshund that can jump up and click its heels on receiving good news
HOT DOG	A dachshund
HOT FLASH	A dachshund either entering or leaving menopause
HOT FOOT	A dachshund that knows when to leave the scene fast
HOT FUDGE	A dachshund that's overweight
HOT LIPS	A dachshund with sex appeal
HOT ROD	A dachshund that runs fast
HOTSHOT	A dachshund that throws its money around
HOT TAMALE	A dachshund from Mexico
HOT TODDY	A dachshund that drinks
HOUDINI	For a disappearing pet
HOUGHTON	For an Irish wolfhound
HOUSTON	For a pet from Texas
HOWARD	For a tawny boxer or Howard Huge
HOWARD HUGHES	For a tawny Great Dane
HOWDY DOODY	A baby boomer's pet
HOWELL	Someone stuck on Gilligan's island
HUBBARD	For a mother
HUBBLE	A dog with great vision
HUBERT	For a basset hound
HUBIE	For cream point Birman
HUCK FINN	A pet that likes to travel, preferably by raft
HUCKLEBERRY HOUND	The favorite cartoon character

HUD	For a very sexy, tough looking yet vulnerable pet
HUDSON	For a fish
HUEY	For anyone whose last name is Lewis
HUGH	For a pug
HUGO	I like it for a Shar-pei
HUMBOLDT	For a harlequin Great Dane
HUMPERDINCK	A singer's pet
HUMPHREY	Great for an Old English sheepdog
HUNT	For a fox
HUNTER	For any hunting animal
HUNTLEY	Brinkley's partner
HURLY	Pair with burly
HURRICANE	A pet that comes from Miami
HUSSEIN	For a King Charles spaniel
HUSSY	The second wife that overlapped the first
HUTCH	A Cairn terrier
HUTCHINGS	An English cocker spaniel
HUTTON	A model pet
HUXFORD	An American foxhound
HUXLEY	For a Scottish terrier

I, CLAUDIUS	For an egocentric pet that looks good in a toga
I.C.U.	For a pet that likes to play peekaboo
I.D.	For a paranoid pet
IAGO	Bad character, watch out
IAN	For a pet with a purpose
IBM	For a pet that can honestly say "I've Been Moved" or, for the more literal-minded, a pet into mainframe computing
IBSEN	For a pet in a doll's house
ICARUS	For someone with an agenda
ICEBERG	For a green, leafy pet
ICE CAP	For a bulldog that wears a hat
ICE CREAM	For a chocolate Labrador retriever
ICE CUBE	For a pet that loves being in the water
ICED TEA	For a pet that likes to sit on the porch
ICELANDER	For a pet that likes skidding across frozen ponds
ICEMAN	For pets who cometh when you calleth
ICHABOD	For a harlequin Great Dane

ID	For a pet with a conscience
IDA	For an English bulldog
IDDY	For an iddy-biddy pet
IDRIS	For a honey mink Tonkinese
IDYLL	For a very idyllic, pastoral pet
IGGY	For a Dandie Dinmont terrier
IGLOO	For an Alaskan malamute . . . what else?
IGNACE	For a van cream Turkish
IGNACOUS	For a Scottish terrier
IGNATIUS	For a giant schnauzer
IGNITE	A pyromaniac's pet
IGOR	What a great name. Russian wolfhound?
IKE	For a Republican
IKEHORN	For a *Scruples* fan
ILANA	For a German wirehaired pointer
ILENE	For an American shorthair
ILIAD	Any pet that likes classics or travel
ILLUSION	When you believe that they've actually gotten trained, and they haven't
ILLUSTRATOR	A pet for an advertising director
ILSE	For a Swedish shepherd
ILYA	For a Russian blue or korat
IMAGINE	For a peaceful pet
IMELDA	Four paws is a good start for a shoe collection
IMMIGRANT	For a foreign pet
IMOGENE	For a coco colored pet
IMP	For a Yorkie

IMPERIAL HIGHNESS	For an Angora
IMPLORER	For a pet that's always begging
IMPORTED	For a foreign breed
IMPORTER	For the person who brought over the imported breed
IMPOSTER	For the pet that pretends to be imported
IMPRESSER	For the pet that pretends to be imported in order to impress
IMPRESSIVE	For the pet that actually is imported and is impressive
IMPULSE	For the owner that would like to strangle the imported impresser
IMUS	For an early morning pet
INA	For a miniature schnauzer
INCA	For a builder
INCH	For a snake
INCORPORATE	For someone with a new pet and a new business
INCUBATOR	For a preemie
INDEPENDENT	For a borzoi
INDEX	For an organized pet
INDIA	For a pet with a spot on its forehead
INDIA INK	For a black pet
INDIAN	For a feathered pet
INDIANA	For an American foxhound
INDIANA JONES	For a pet that likes adventure
INDIAN SUMMER	For a golden retriever or any pet that thrives in autumn
INDIC	For a wetterhoun

INDICATOR	For a pet that gives you a hint before biting
INDIGO	For a blue pet
INDIRA	For a female leader of pets
INDISCREET	For a tomcat
INDOCHINE	For a Siamese
INDOOR	My cat ... the only outdoor cat that comes inside to go to the bathroom ... where did I go wrong?
INDY	For a pet that likes adventure
INERTIA	For a pet that won't move unless provoked
INES	For a Catalan sheepdog
INEXHAUSTIBLE	For a Dandie Dinmont terrier
INEZ	A fabulous pet name
INFERNO	For a towering pet
INFIELDER	For a ball chaser
INFINITY	For a driving pet
INFLICTER	For a pit bull, doberman, rottweiler, etcetera
INFLIGHT	For a cockatoo
INFORMANT	For a parrot
INFORMER	For a parakeet
INFRADIP	For a pet that likes to swim
INFRARED	For a bat
INGLEBERT	For a Javanese
INGMAR	For a drever, a dog also known as a Swedish dachsbracke, or a director's pet
INGOT	For a pet as good as gold
INGRAM	For someone who listens to WCBS in New York City or is into books

INGRID	For a Swedish hound
INGROWN	A podiatrist's pet
INKBERRY	For a black and white Persian
INKBLOTZ	A psychiatrist's pet
INKLE	For an American curl
INKLING	For someone who doesn't quite get it
INKSPOT	A printer's pet
INKWELL	For a black Bombay
INNER CIRCLE	For a pet in the in crowd
INNER SPACE	For a pet that wants its own territory
INNIE	Outie's brother
INNING	A baseball fan's pet
INNIS	A pet for a Roy
INOCULATOR	A doctor's pet
INPUT	A computer operator's pet
INSIDE OUT	For a Devon rex
INSIDER	A trader's pet
INSIDE TRACK	For a greyhound
INSOLE	Another podiatrist's pet
INSOMNIA	For a nocturnal pet
INSOMNIAC	For an aggressive nocturnal pet
INSPECTOR	For a Clouseau fan
INSPIRATION	A photographer's pet
INSTALLER	A cable TV man's pet
INSTALLMENT	For an expensive pet
INSTINCT	For your basic pet
INSTRUCTOR	For a bossy pet
INSURANCE	Instead of a burglar alarm
INSURED	For a very expensive pet

INTEGRATED	For a black and white pet
INTERIM	The pet you buy before having the baby
INTERLOPER	For a pet that constantly jumps in bed with you at the wrong moments
INTERMEZZO	An opera lover's pet
INTERNAL REVENUE	An auditor's pet
INTERNATION	Good name for a mutt
INTERPOL	A spy's pet
INTERROGATE	For a Staffordshire bull terrier ... your simple pit bull type
INTESTINE	A snake
INTREPID	A sailor's pet
INTRO	For your first pet
INTUITION	A psychic's pet
INVENTOR	A storyteller's pet
INVESTOR	A pet for a Wall Street tycoon
INVISIBLE MAN	For the pet that's never there when you want it ... and *is* when you don't
INXS	For a large pet
IODINE	For any red pet
IONESCO	A playwright's pet ... on the absurd side
IOTA	For someone who can't afford the whole thing (Toyota)
IPANEMA	For a pet that's soft, and tan, and ... lovely, the girl from Ipanema goes walking
IQ	A pet that tests well
IRA	For a pet that looks like an accountant

IRELAND	An Irish wolfhound's dream
IRENE	American foxhound
IRENEE	American foxhound with a whine
IRIS	An opthalmologist's pet
IRISH	For an Irish setter
IRISH STEW	For the setter's litter
IRMA	For an American wirehair
IRMA LA DOUCE	For a longhaired dachshund
IRON	A bulldog that likes to flex its muscles
IRON AGE	For the bulldog that's a little old-fashioned
IRONCLAD	For the bulldog you'll never get out of owning
IRON CURTAIN	For the bulldog that's out of touch
IRON JOHN	For the bulldog that knows he's a real man
IRON MAN	For the bulldog that lifts weights
IRONWEED	For a mutt that aspires to be a bulldog
IRON WILL	For the bulldog that's won the battle over who's master
IRON WOOD	For the bulldog that golfs
IRONY	For a person who really didn't want the bulldog but now loves it
IROQUOIS	For an American eagle
IRS	For someone who's constantly audited
IRV	Irving's nickname
IRVING	What a fabulous name for a pet
IRVIS	The father was Irving and the mother was Mavis

IRWIN	Also a good name for any pet
ISAAC	For a mellow cat, or for the pet of a violin player
ISABELL	For the parrot that chimes in
ISABELLA	A pet that likes explorers
ISADORA	A lovely, independent cat
ISADORA DUNCAN	For a cat that leaps, or a dunker (a dog from Norway)
ISAIAH	For any pet that foretells the future
ISHERWOOD	For any pet that treats life as a cabaret
ISHIKAWA	For a Japanese bobtail
ISHKABIBBLE	For a pet that's too cute for a real name
ISHMAEL	For a whale watcher
ISHTAR	For a camel watcher
ISIDORE	For a pet that thinks it's a door (for a pet that lets you in and out)
ISLAND QUEEN	For a pet from Manhattan
ISOLDA	A salesman's pet
ISSEY	For a cockney, hissing animal
ISUZU	For a pet that would say anything to make a sale
ITCH	An allergic person's pet
ITCHY	For a prickly pet
ITHACA	For someone who likes cold winters
ITURBI	A concert pianist's pet
IVAN	For a male pet who's terrible but not that terrible
IVAN THE TERRIBLE	For a male pet who IS that terrible

IVANA	For a female pet who's terrible but not that terrible
IVANA THE TERRIBLE	For the female pet who IS that terrible
IVANHOE	I read it, but I don't remember what it was about
IVES	A burly pet
IVOR	A Russian wolfhound
IVORY	For any white pet where a tusk is a plus
IVY	For a Boston terrier
IVY LEAGUE	For a Boston terrier with credentials
IZOD	For a preppie pet . . . unless you have an alligator
IZZY	For a pet partial to homemade chicken soup

J.D.   For a delinquent pet

J. EDGAR   For an American bloodhound

JABBA   For a big, fat pet

JABBAR   For a basketball fan

JABBERWOCKY   For a Lewis Carroll fan

JABOT   A pet with a crest of white hair at the neck

JACK   The most-used name for the Jack Russell terrier

JACK BENNY   For a penny-pinching Jack Russell

JACK FROST   For a northern Jack Russell

JACKHAMMER   For a loud Jack Russell

JACKIE   For a female Jack Russell

JACKKNIFE   For a tough Jack Russell

JACK LONDON   For a literary Jack Russell

JACKO   For a circus Jack Russell

JACKPOT   For a gambler's Jack Russell

JACKRABBIT   For a quick Jack Russell

JACKSON   For a Browne pet

JACOB   For a religious pet

JACOBY	For a litigious pet ... pair with Meyers
JACQUARD	A fabric manufacturer's pet
JACQUELINE	For a black and white American curl longhair
JACQUETTA	For a pet that wears a jacket
JACUZZI	For a pet that appreciates the good life
JADE	For a bichon avanese ... small dog, plesant but rare companion
JADED	For a bichon avanese that's been around
JAEGER	For an English setter ... well dressed and sporty
JAFFEE	For a Sam or a Rona
JAGGER	For a Rolling Stones fan
JAI ALAI	For a Spanish mastiff that fetches
JAIME	For a nonpedigree blue and white shorthair
JAKE	One of my favorites ... for humans as well as animals
JALAPEÑO	This one's a pepper
JALOPY	For a floppy pet, or one that loves to ride in the car
JAM	A musician's pet
JAMAL	For a Rhodesian ridgeback
JAMBALAYA	For a mixed breed
JAMBOREE	For a pet that likes to march
JAMEEL	For a basketball fan
JAMES	For a formal pet
JAMES BOND	For a spy pet
JAMES BROWN	For a singing pet

JAMES DEAN	For a rebel pet
JAMIE	For a halfhearted rebel pet
JAMMER	For a windy pet
JAMMIES	For the pet that sleeps a lot
JAM SESSION	A musician's brood
JAMSHID	Early legendary king of Persia
JAN	Pair with Dean
JANA	For a Pyrenees mastiff ... big and powerful, friendly and doesn't eat much
JANE	See Jane. See Jane run.
JANEANE	For someone into double single names
JANE DOE	For a pet from the humane society
JANE EYRE	A pet with a sense of melodrama and expressive eyes ... pair with Mr. Rochester
JANE MARPLE	For an old bloodhound
JANET	For a good, reliable animal ... one that won't let you down
JANGLE	For a Tennessee treeing brindle
JANGLES	Mr. Bo
JANIE	A sweet and pretty pet
JANOVIC	For a person into decorating
JANUARY	For an Aquarian
JANUARY MAN	For a police dog
JANUS	For a guard dog
JAPHETH	Son of Noah
JARGON	For a mixed breed
JARRAH	An Australian tree ... for one of your larger breeds

JARRED	For a trigg hound . . . created in Kentucky for hunting
JARRUS	For a hovawart . . . runs easily over difficult terrain
JARVIS	A black and tan coonhound
JASMINE	For a basenji or any exotic pet
JASON	For the pet with a golden fleece
JASPER	A Johns pet
JASSID	For a pet that likes arid, hot climates
JASTROW	For a Chesapeake Bay retriever
JAT	A pet for a Punjabi
JAVA	For someone who loves coffee, or any dark brown pet
JAWS	Nice for a rottweiler
JAY	For a jaybird
JAYBIRD	For a blue jay, Mexican hairless, or Devon rex (also hairless)
JAYNE	A fancy Jane
JAYNE MANSFIELD	For a young bichon frise
JAZEMOND	For a pet with airs
JAZMINE	For a pet that smells good
JAZZ	For a hot, cool pet
JEAN	For a pet in its prime
JEANETTE	For a tortie and white Scottish fold
JEAN-MARIE	A parochial school pet
JEANNIE	For the pet you dream of
JEANS	For any of the blue pets
JEDI	For a pet that battles interstellar evil
JEDIDIAH	For a peaceful pet

JEDI KNIGHT	For a Doberman, rottweiler, or Newfoundland
JEEP	For a pet willing to travel anywhere
JEEVES	The butler's pet
JEFFERSON	For a presidential pet
JEFFREY	Jefferson's nickname
JEHOSHAPHAT	For a pet frog
JEKYLL	Hyde's pal
JELL-O	For a pudgy, roly-poly pet
JELLY	For a very cuddly, soft, fat pet
JELLY BEAN	A pet for Ronald Reagan
JELLY ROLL	For a dachshund
JENA	For a Somerset harrier
JENKINS	Sounds more like a butler
JENNELL	For a Swedish shepherd
JENNINGS	For someone who likes to watch the evening news
JENNY	For a Maltese
JENSEN	For a pet that likes silverware
JEOPARDY	For the quiz show fanatic, or for a guard dog
JEREMIA	Was a bullfrog
JEREMIAH	Was a good friend of mine
JEREMY	For a pet with its irons in the fire
JERMAINE	For a singing and dancing pet
JEROME	For an Old English sheepdog
JERRELL	For a wild Abyssinian
JERRY	A pal for Tom
JESSE	My own wonderful son, but, still a good name for your pet
JESSE JAMES	For a rascal

JESSEL	For a comedian and toastmaster's pet
JESSUP	For a Pyrenees mastiff
JESTER	For a Maltese with a bow in its hair
JET	For a black pet
JET LAG	For a pet who sleeps a lot
JET SET	For three Afghans
JETH	For a tawny boxer
JETHRO	For a fan of ''The Beverly Hillbillies''
JETSAM	Another pet from the pound
JETTY	For a Portuguese or Irish water dog
JEWEL	For any priceless pet
JEWELS	For someone in the family
JEZEBEL	For a female pet that flirts
JEZEBELLE	For a very forward, nondiscriminatory pet
JIANG	For a Shih Tzu
JIFFY	For a racing animal
JIGS	For a work dog
JIGSAW	For a puzzling pet
JIING DONG	For a Lhasa apso or any Asian pet
JILL	Pair for a Jack Russell terrier
JILLIAN	Isn't this a great name for any female pet?
JIM DANDY	A pet that's an excellent example of its breed
JIMENEZ	For José
JIMINEY CRICKET	Walt Disney's character in *Pinocchio*
JIMMY	For a pet with a large beak or a very long snout

JIMMY STEWART	For an Afghan
JINX	For a black cat
JITTERBUG	For a chihuahua, toy poodle, or anything else small and hyper
JO	One of the *Little Women*
JOANIE	"Happy Days"
JOAN OF ARC	Not so "Happy Days"
JOB	A pet with problems
JOBBER	A middleman's pet
JOBLESS	A pure luxury pet
JOCASTA	Queen of Thebes and mother of Oedipus
JOCK	An athlete's pet
JOCKEY	For a pet that likes to go to the races
JODHPUR	For a pet that likes to go to the races and wear pants
JODHPURR	For a cat that likes to go to the races, wear pants, and ride horses
JODI	For a Pekingese
JOE	For a dependable pet like Janet
JOEL	For a Grey pet
JOE LEWIS	A pet for a boxing fan
JOE MONTANA	A pet for a football fan
JOE PALOOKA	A fictional pet for a boxing fan
JOEY	For an American shorthair
JOFFREY	A pet for a ballet lover
JOHN	Another American shorthair
JOHN DOE	For a pet from the pound
JOHN HANCOCK	A pet for a scribe

JOHN HENRY	A steel-driving pet
JOHNNY	A pet that drinks out of the toilet
JOHNNY ON TIME	For a pet that is well trained
JOHNSON	For a Turkish van
JOIE	For a happy French pet
JOIE DE VIVRE	For a happy French pet that loves life
JOINT CHIEF	For a bulldog
JO JO	Jo's pet name
JOJOBA	For a clean pet
JOKER	For a practical joker
JOLLY	For a happy American pet
JOLLY RANCHER	For a happy American pet with a ranch
JOLLY ROGER	For a happy pet ... always raiding the refrigerator like a pirate
JOLSON	For someone who loves his mammy
JONAH	For the largest fish in the tank
JONAS	A pet that appreciates the meaning of vaccines
JONATHAN	Once a rarely seen breed. Now everyone has one.
JONES	For a pet that likes to use an alias
JONESES	A pet you try to keep up with
JONESIE	A pet you're immediately comfortable with
JONG	For a pet that has a fear of flying
JON JON	For a small Jon
JONQUIL	A yellow-haired pet
JOON	A Japanese bobtail
JOPLIN	For an American longhair

A pet from Kansas City, short for kitty cat, or a pet from a sunshine band	
For a silent pet with a white face	
For a Hungarian communist	
For a borzoi	
For a pharaoh hound	
For a Hawaiian pet	
For someone who likes rolls	
A journalist's pet	
For the fish tank	
For a collie	
Another pharaoh hound	
Mongolian language	
An after dinner pet	
Hindu god of love	
For a very with it, trend setting pet	
For a hyperactive pet	
A painter's pet	
A chocoholic's pet	
For a dancing pet	

SCOPE

JORDACHE	A jeans person's pet
JORDAN	Pair with Marsh . . . a shopper's pet
JORDANA	One of Jackie Collins' newest characters so good for any pet or pet owner into melodrama
JORDIE	For a small shopper
JOREL	Superman's father. Good for a pet used for breeding
JORGE	A Spanish George
JOSÉ	A Spanish Joe
JOSEPH	For a pet that dreams in Technicolor
JOSEPHINA	A Spanish Josephine
JOSEPHINE	An English Josephina
JOSETTE	A French bulldog
JOSHUA	For a colorpointed European Devon rex
JOSLYN	For an Angora, or any pet that's really girly
JOSS	For someone who believes in luck
JOSYLEN	A lucky lady
JOURNEYMAN	A traveler's pet
JOWLS	Basset hounds and bulldogs
JOY	A happy pet
JOYCE	A happy pet that writes
JOYCLYN	A happy pet that brings good fortune
JOYFUL	A happy pet that brings good fortune and good health
JOYRIDE	A happy pet large enough for your child to ride on
JUAN	A Spanish John
JUAN CARLOS	King of Spain

JUANITA	A Spanish Jane
JUÁREZ	Mexican national hero (1806–1872)
JUBILEE	You received this pet for a big anniversary
JUDAH	For a Maccabees
JUDAS	For a pit bull
JUDD	A country singer's pet
JUDE	Hey
JUDGE	A pet for a juror
JUDITH	Cary Grant would never have been able to repeat it three times in a row like Judy
JUDO	For a martial arts buff
JUDSON	Judd's full name
JUDY	Judy, Judy, Judy!
JUGHEAD	For an Archie comic fan
JUGO	For someone into juice (Spanish)
JUICER	For someone into health food
JUILLIARD	For a very talented pet
JUJUBEE	For someone into junk food
JUKEBOX	For someone into the fifties
JULEP	For someone into mint drinks
JULES	For someone into Feiffer
JULIA	For someone into Roberts
JULIANA	For an Egyptian mau
JULIET	Romeo, oh, Romeo . . .
JULIO	For a springer spaniel . . . I like the incongruity of it
JULIUS	For someone into the color orange
JULIUS CAESAR	For someone into power
JULY	For a July baby

JUMBO	For a big baby
JUMPING JACK	Another Jack Russe
JUMP SHOT	A basketball player
JUNE	For a June baby
JUNG	For someone into
JUNGLE JIM	For a Jim that lik
JUNGLE SPIRIT	For a Jim that us
JUNIUS	I don't get it my
JUNO	For an Alaskan
JUPITER	For a "Norther any one into o
JURA	For a Turkish
JURASSIC	For a frog
JUROR	A trial attorne
JURY	A trial attorn pet
JUSTIN	A harlequin my eldest s
JUSTINE	A female h
JUSTIN THYME	A harlequi cook
JUTE	Hey

K.C.

KABUK
KÁDÁR
KAFKA
KAHLIL
KAHUN
KAISER
KALB
KALEIDO
KALI
KALIB
KALMUK
KALUHA
KAMA
KAMALI
KAMIKAZE
KANDINSK
KANDYMA
KAN KAN

KANNADA	A language from southern India
KANSAS	For a family moving from Kansas (a Cairn terrier)
KAPPA	For a fraternity aficionado
KARA	Mia mine
KARAMAZOV	For brothers
KARATE	A martial arts aficionado's pet
KARATE KID	The child of the martial arts aficionado's pet
KAREEM	Better than milk for your cat
KARLOFF	Boris' pal
KARMA	For the pet that was meant to be
KARRAS	For a very big pet
KARTIK	Hindu month
KARTOOSH	For a silver Egyptian mau
KARUS	A character from *Bambi*
KASEY	A fancy Casey
KASHA	For a Varnisha. For you folks out there, this is a noodle dish.
KASHMIR	The territory, not the cloth
KASPER	A designer's pet
KASPI	For someone with fond memories of the Caspian Sea
KASSANDRA	A beautiful, full, fluffy feline
KASSIE	For a calico longhair
KAT	A fancy Cat
KATARINA	For a Russian blue
KATE	Katherine's nickname
KATEEBA	An Egyptian mau shorthair
KATERINA	A Russian blue shorthair
KATHERINE	A calico American shorthair

KATIE	A nonpedigree American shorthair
KATMANDOO	A male cat's litter box
KATO	A pet that's a real trial
KATONA	A beagle
KATRINA	A borzoi . . . docile and extremely loyal
KATSUMI	Just what you don't want your cat to do
KATZ	For a dog
KAVA	The beginnings of a trip to the dentist
KAVANAGH	For an Irish setter without cavities
KAVIDA	A dentist's pet
KAY	For a Cairn terrier
KAYAK	For an Alaskan malamute
KAYE	For a Danny fan
KAYOED	For a boxer
KAZZI	A chocolate tortie Persian
KEANU	For a speedy pet
KEATON	For a Buster, Diane, or Michael fan
KEATS	Poet
KEELER	For a boater or a dancer, or someone into rubies
KEEN	For a pet from the fifties
KEEPER	When you weren't sure, but went for it
KEFAUVER	For a political animal
KEFIR	A drink made from fermented cow's milk
KEGLER	A bowler's pet
KEIKO	Japanese bobtail
KELB	Means ''dog'' in Arabic

KELLOGG	For a cereal pet
KELLY	An Irish springer spaniel
KELVIN	A blue Korat
KEMP	A champion
KEN	Pair with Barbie
KENDALL	For a dog that looks like a Ken doll
KENDL	For an altered Ken doll dog
KENDRIX	For a lavender Abyssinian
KENJI	For a Japanese spitz
KENNETH	For an aspiring hairdresser
KENO	À la Bingo
KENT	An aspiring duke or duchess' pet
KENTON	A Sussex spaniel
KENTUCKY BUS	For a greyhound
KENTUCKY D	For a very fast horse
KENTUCKY DERBY	For someone who likes racing
KENYA	For a New York Marathon winner
KENYATTA	Kenya's first president (1964–1978)
KENZO	A designing pet
KERBY	For a Cosmo Topper fan
KERMIT	For a green pet
KERNEL	For a teeny-weeny pet
KERRIA	For a Croatian sheepdog
KERRY	For an English sheepdog
KERRY BLUE	For the cat
KETCH	For a retriever
KETCHUP	For a red pet, or one that's always late

KEVIN	For a pet that likes bacon
KEWPIE DOLL	An Angora ... what could be Kewpier?
KEYBOARD	A pianist's pet
KEYNOTE	A speaker's pet
KEYS	A musician's pet
KGB	A Russian spy's pet
KHAFRE	Egyptian pharaoh
KHAKI	For an American army pet
KHALID	King of Saudi Arabia
KHALKHA	Official language of the Mongolian People's Republic
KHASHOGGI	For someone into money
KIBBE	For someone who likes Arabic food
KIBBI	For a little, round, puffy dog, like a bichon frise
KICKING BEAR	A Bernese mountain dog, Newfoundland ... something really *big*
KIDD	For a young pet
KIDDER	For someone very Margo
KIDDISH	For a pet that acts young, or one that likes to eat on Saturday afternoons
KIERKEGAARD	For a philosophical animal
KILDARE	For a pet that aspires to be a doctor
KILEY	For an Australian terrier ... lively, spirited, and dignified
KILO	A dieter's pet, or a weight lifter's pet
KILROY	Was here
KIM	A jungle animal (*see* Kipling)
KIMOSABE	Tonto's pet name for the Lone Ranger
KING	Perfect name for any big dog

KING CHARLES	How could I pass up placing a King Charles spaniel right here?
KING EDWARD	For an English mastiff
KINGFISH	From the ''Amos and Andy'' TV series
KING GEORGE	For a harlequin Great Dane
KING HUSSEIN	For a Neapolitan mastiff
KING KONG	For a pug
KING LOUIS	For your fourteenth pet
KING-SIZE	For an English mastiff
KINSKI	Nastassja and Klaus, for when you've kept the offspring
KIOWA	For a blue Tonkinese
KIPLING	Gunga Din, Rudyard, Kim
KIPLINGER	For someone into newsletters
KIPPY	For a smooth collie
KIR	Saint Bernards seem to get all the ''liquor'' names
KIRI	For a field spaniel ... hardy and fast, sweet and affectionate
KIRK	For a Trekkie
KIRKPATRICK	For an ambassador
KIRKWOOD	For a funny cat
KIRMAN	For someone who likes Persian rugs
KIRSTEN	For a pet that will evenually make a debut
KISHI	For a Lhasa apso
KISHKA	Another name for a hyperactive pet
KISMET	For the pet that was meant to be
KISSES	For a pet that loves to lick

KISSINGER	For a German shorthaired pointer. So good at negotiating his position, he might win the Nobel Peace Prize.
KIT	For a "Knight Rider" fan
KITT	For an earthy pet
KITTEN	Actually, a very sweet name ... also Kathy's nickname from "Father Knows Best"
KITTY	For a "Gunsmoke" fan
KITTYHAWK	Flying cats
KIWI	For someone into fruit or shoe polish
KLAUS	For someone into Germans
KLEE	For someone into art
KLEIST	For someone into German war history
KLEMPERER	For someone into "Hogan's Heroes"
KLINGER	For someone into "M*A*S*H"
KLONDIKE	For someone into bars
KLUTE	For a detective
KNICK	For a pet that can jump through hoops
KNICKERBOCKER	For a pet that can jump through hoops and drink beer at the same time
KNIEVEL	For an evil pet, or a pet that jumps cars
KNIGHT RIDER	For a pet that rides at night
KNISH	For a pet into potatoes
KNOCKWURST	For a dachshund
KNOEDLER	An art lover's pet
KNOX	For a pet with good strong nails, or built like a fort
KOCCHI	For an Italian pointer
KOCH	For a mayoral candidate

KODACHROME	A photographer's pet
KODAK	For a picture perfect pet
KOKOLADA	For someone who likes to vacation in the islands
KONG	For a big, hairy gorilla
KOOKY	For a crazy pet
KOPPEL	For a pet that needs a new hairstyle
KORNELIA	An opthalmologist's pet
KORNY	For a pet with eye problems
KOUFAX	For any pet that can make a record number of strikeouts in one season
KOWTOW	A yes-man's pet
KRAKATOA	For a big pet that steps on your foot all the time
KRAMER	A Dandie Dinmont terrier, or for a ''Seinfeld'' fan
KRAUS	For a German pet
KREPLACH	For a Yiddish pet
KRIS	*See* Kristofferson
KRISPIE	For a pet into rice cakes
KRISTIE	For an Irish terrier
KRISTOFFLE	Christofle with a K ... someone into silver
KRISTOFFERSON	A name that will only appear on its pedigree papers ... otherwise, it's Kris to the family
KROOK	For a pet who steals ... for a krooked crook
KRUPA	For someone who loves music, especially drums
KRYSTLE	A pet for a Carrington

KUBLAI KHAN	For any of the Chinese pets with a talent for running an empire
KUBRICK	For someone looking forward to the year 2001
KURALT	For a pet that likes to travel around the United States
KURTZ	Swoosie Kurtz ... now there's a name for you!
KYM	For a Kim that likes to go to the gym for a swim with him and Jim
KYOTO	For any of the Japanese breeds

L. L. BEAN	For a catalog shopper
LABELLE	For a beautiful French pointer
LACE	For a cavalier King Charles spaniel
LACES	For the cat that's always playing with your shoes
LACEY	Cagney's partner
LACOYNA	For a Croatian sheepdog
LAD	Male collie
LADDIE	Male collie's son
LADDIE BOY	Any pet whose owner has Irish eyes
LADIBYRD	No, it's not named after the former first lady
LADY	Tramp's girlfriend
LADY BIRD	This one is
LADY CHATTERLEY'S LOVER	A pet who sleeps with you
LADY DI	For a pet with a lot of baggage
LADY JANE	For an Old English mastiff
LADY MACBETH	Dalmatians. Out, damned spot!

LAFAYETTE	French poodles
LA FEMME NIKITA	For a female that *really* knows how to take care of herself
LAFITTE	An expensive pet
LAGERFELD	A designer's pet
LAILA	Will ease your worried mind
LAKE	For a Portuguese water dog
LA LA	I actually know someone named La La. It's so cute.
LAMARR	For a Hedy pet
LAMB	A Bedlington terrier
LAMBCHOP	For someone who grew up with Shari Lewis
LAMBIE PIE	For someone who grew up with my mother
L'AMOUR	For someone in love with love
LANCASTER	For those who like to go for midnight swims
LANCE	Lancelot's nickname
LANCELOT	For a *Camelot* fan
LANDERS	For a pet that gives advice
LANDON	For a pet that thinks it's a pilot
LAND ROVER	For a family that has the car and the pet that roams free
LANDY	For a Lakeland terrier . . . affectionate, cheerful, and stubborn
LANG	For a Ronettes fan . . . do lang, do lang, do lang
LANGFORD	For a viszla . . . intelligent and trainable, a hunting dog
LANGLEY	A CIA agent's pet
LANGSTON	A poet's pet

LANGTRY	A dog who lives west of the Rockies
LANIE	A nice, plump Himalayan
LANSBURY	For a "Murder, She Wrote" fan
LANSING	For a female movie aficionado
LANVIN	For a pet that smells great
LANZA	Perfect for a singing Mario
LAPIS	For a pet into gems, or one with fur that gleams
LAPIS LAZULI	For a gem
LAPTOP	For someone with both the cat and the computer
LAREDO	A pet with a western emphasis
LARSEN	My accountant, or any Scandinavian pet
LASSIE	Collies. What else?
LATKA	"Taxi"
LA TOYA	For a pet with a lot of siblings
LAUDER	A pet with good skin
LAUGHTON	For a basset hound. Remember Charles Laughton?
LAUPER	For a pet with orange hair
LAURA	An American shorthair . . . like Laura Petrie
LAURA ASHLEY	Clothes designer
LAUREL	Pair with Hardy
LAUREN	Clothes designer
LAURENCE OLIVIER	For an Egyptian sphynx, or any pet that puts on a good show
LAURENT	Clothes designer
LAURI	Clothes wearer
LAVERNE	And Shirley

LAWFORD	A presidential brother-in-law type
LAWRENCE	An animal who won't loosen up
LAYAWAY	For an expensive pet
LAYOFF	For one of the nonworking breeds
LAYOUT	An art designer's pet
LAZULI	Another beautiful pet name, pair with Lapis
LEA	Twentieth century version of biblical name
LEAH	A biblical name for a religious pet
LEAHY	Irish setter, Irish wolfhound, etcetera
LEAR	A Seeing Eye dog
LEARY	Heavy doses of catnip
LEBEAU	Hogan's French friend
LE CARRÉ	A spy dog
LEE	A Confederate pet
LEEWAY	A pet for whom you keep having to make exceptions
LEFTY	For an animal with two left feet (all of them!)
LEGEND	For any animal with a mink coat
LE GRAND	A very large animal that reminds you of a sports car
LEHMAN	More brothers
LEIF	A Norwegian elkhound
LELAND	For an "L. A. Law" fan
LEMONADE	For a sourpuss
LENDL	For a tennis fan
LENIN	For a Siberian husky
LENNON	For an English setter with a talent for composing

LENNY	For a comedian
LENO	For an NBC late nighter
LENYA	For a Lotte
LEO	For a large cat, or pet born in August
LEON	One of the great names
LEONA	From rags to riches to the pen
LEONARD	My lawyer
LEONARDO	A Teenage Mutant Ninja Turtle, or someone into real art
LEONORE	For a flat-coated retriever
LEOTA	For an Iceland dog ... lively, affectionate, and active
LESLIE	An animal of indeterminate gender
LESTER	Great for a golden retriever, don't you think?
LETTERMAN	For a CBS late nighter
LETTY	A feminist's pet
LEVANT	Talented but alcoholic
LEVI'S	Blue pets
LEWIS	And Clark ... for the pair that likes to explore the neighborhood
LIABLE	An attorney's pet
LIAM	Big and beautiful
LIBBY	A pet that likes canned peas
LIBERACE	For a pet with great flair and panache
LIBERTY	Truth, justice, and the American way
LICHTENSTEIN	A painter's pet
LICKERISH	For the pet that thinks that you're the candy
LICORICE	A candy lover's pet

LIGHTFOOT	For that pet that manages to sneak up on you every time
LIGHTNING	Female half of a Great Dane couple (*See* "Doubles," Thunder and Lightning)
L'IL ABNER	A backwoods pet
LILAC	Smells like a room freshener
LILAH	For a lilac lynx point Javanese
LILI	High Lili, high low
LILITH	"Cheers" and "Frasier" . . . a pit bull
LILY	A pet of the valley
LIMA BEAN	A pet that's good for you
LIMBAUGH	For a big, opinionated pet . . . preferably Republican
LIMBO	For a pet unsure of its next move
LIMOGES	Delicate and expensive
LIN YI	A chow chow, Lhasa apso, Shih Tzu, etcetera
LINCOLN	For a bearded, honest pet
LINDA	The name of a good girl
LINDBERGH	Birds
LINDFORS	Better for a butler than a pet
LINDSAY	My niece's name
LINKLETTER	An artful pet
LINUS	A pet with a blanket
LION	For a pet that's not afraid to take what it wants
LIONEL	For a male into trains
LIONELLE	For a female into trains
LIPOSUCTION	Greyhounds

LIPPI	Artist
LIPPIE	For someone into collagen injections
LIPS	For a snake
LIPSTICK	For a femme fatale
LISZT	A composer's pet
LITHGOW	An actor's pet
LITTLE BIG MAN	For a pug
LITTLE JOHN	Big John's son
LITTLE LORD FAUNTLEROY	For a pet you plan to dress up
LITTLE LOTTA	A fat boxer
LITTLE RICHARD	Good golly, Miss Molly
LIVERWURST	Dalmatians
LIVINGSTON	Always wandering off
LIZ	*See* "Doubles," Liz and Richard
LIZA	Long legs, short hair, pedigree lineage
LIZZIE	For a snake, unless you get a lizard
LLOYD	For a basset hound
LOAFER	For all cats
LOFTY	For a pet that's full of itself
LOGAN	A pet you picked up at Boston's airport
LOIS	Pair with Clark
LOIS LANE	Professional suffering from unrequited love
LOLA	Sexy but not too sexy
LOLLI	Your two-year-old's pronunciation
LOLLICAT	Your three-year-old's choice
LOLLIPOP	Your four-year-old's wish

LOLLIPUP	Your self-congratulatory solution
LOLLOBRIGIDA	Everyone will know what you meant
LOMBARD	Blond and beautiful
LOMBARDI	Powerful and competitive
LOMBARDO	For a guy
LONDON	For any of the English breeds
LONGFELLOW	A dachshund
LONGSHOT	A dachshund that races
LONGWORTH	The dachshund that wins
LONI	For a pet smarter than it looks
LOOFAH	For a bristly pet
LOPEZ	Trini
LORD BYRON	For an Old English sheepdog, English mastiff, etcetera
LOREN	For a Dandie Dinmont terrier . . . a great mouse catcher, affectionate, and playful
LORENZO	My cousin Ruth's new husband
LORETTA	For an ordinary tabby. What a great cat name!
LORRE	For a Peter
LOTTE	Lenya
LOU ELLA	Happens to be a matchmaker in New York City
LOU ELLEN	Happens to be a client
LOUIE	You'd better love the song
LOUIS	Would like to be a client
LOUIS VUITTON	For any pet that has LV LV LV LV LV all over it
LOUISA MAY	Alcott fan's pet

LOUISE	The Pekingese ... great pet name ... makes it seem human
LOUPI	A brown tabby and white Norwegian forest longhair
LOVE	As long as it's not what you call anyone else in the family
LOVE BUG	For a Herbie
LOVE CHILD	A coupling you never approved of but couldn't prevent. Perfect for a mutt
LOVEJOY	For a pet into antiques and mysteries
LOVEY	A red mackerel tabby shorthair
LOWBOY	For a short pet, or a depressed male
LUCA	A pet that needs a good home
LUCAS	See Lukas
LUCCI	For a soap opera buff
LUCE	A pet that sees the light
LUCIA	For a quiet pet
LUCIFER	For a little devil
LUCILLE	Red haired and funny
LUCINDA	For a black cat
LUCKY	For a pet adopted from the pound
LUCKY LUCIA	A hit man's pet
LUCREZIA	For a borzoi, or maybe a pet that eliminates its rivals
LUCY	If you love her
LUDWIG	For a Deutsche dogge
LUGER	A pet for someone in the NRA
LUGOSI	For a molto Bela pet
LUIGI	For an Italian pointer
LUI LUI	"I said, ah, we gotta go"
LUKAS	Sounds like a tough guy to me

LUKE	A semiwarm pet
LUKE SKYWALKER	*Star Wars* . . . any pet that learns tricks the hard way
LULU	For a blue-eyed white Angora
LUMET	For a movie buff
LURCH	For a pet that lopes instead of runs
LUTHER	Devilish
LYLE	Cockatoo, cockatiel, or a crocodile
LYNDON	Definitely perfect for a basset hound
LYON	For a French hound . . . as in the town

MABEL	I don't know why, but I love this name for a pet.
MACARONI	A pet that's a real noodle
MACAROON	A tortoiseshell Persian
MACARTHUR	A pet that likes the park
MACAW	A Hanover hound . . . searches out game, obedient and affectionate
MACBETH	"Out, damned spot!" I guess we know what happened at this house.
MACGREGOR	Perfect for a Scottie, but not too original
MACHO MAN	A pug
MACIVOR	A pet that knows how to use its hands . . . er, paws
MACK	A boxer
MACKENZIE	An English setter
MACKINTOSH	Any pet that likes to go out in the rain
MACK THE KNIFE	A boxer with dangerous claws
MACLEISH	For a pet that doesn't need a leash
MACMURRAY	A pet for someone with three sons

MADAME BOVARY	Any pet into Flaubert
MADELINE	Two Madelines come to mind—the famous one from Paris and one of my mother's friends
MADISON	Pet for a person who adores shopping
MADONNA	The outrageous superstar where anything goes . . . any flamboyant pet
MAE	A big, fat cat . . . I don't think Mae West would mind
MAFIA	For a tough guy pet
MAGEE	A springer spaniel
MAGELLAN	Sailed around the world . . . I suppose a wanderer
MAGGIE	Such a sweet name for a pet. I like it for something big, like a standard poodle or a golden retriever.
MAGIC	This one speaks for itself
MAGNOLIA	A lovely tree that blossoms in early spring . . . also very messy
MAGNUM	Who can look at this word and not think of Tom Selleck?
MAHLER	Composer's pet
MAID MARIAN	Robin Hood's girlfriend
MAILER	A postman's pet
MAIN LINE	Sounds like a bloodhound
MAINE MAN	A pet from Maine. Perfect for a Maine coon
MAIZIE	A female name that is another one of the greats
MAJOR	When the decision wasn't easy
MAJOR LEAGUE	Any pet that costs over four hundred dollars

MA KETTLE	For an old, skinny pet married to Pa
MALCOLM X	A bullmastiff
MALCOME	An Irish wolfhound
MALIBU	For a pet that loves the ocean, as well as the elements
MALLORY	A pet for people with family ties
MALTED	A fluffy cat, or a Maltese
MALTESE FALCON	What else? A Maltese
MAMBO	Another good name for a dachshund
MAMIE	Someone who lived in the White House in the fifties. Great pet name
MAMMA	A nice, fat cat
MANDRAKE	A plant with purplish to white flowers . . . makes me think of a Great Dane
MANET	Artist's pet
MANFRED	For a German hunting terrier
MANGO	For a sloppy pet
MANLY	A German shepherd
MANNA	For the best pet you ever had in your life
MANNY	A smooth fox terrier
MANOLO	A Portuguese water dog . . . they are nonallergic, by the way.
MANSFIELD	Jayne comes to mind, but Mansfield is a wonderful name for a male pet.
MANTRA	For the pet with supernatural powers, or one that repeats the same sound over and over
MAO TSE-TUNG	For a pet that leans to the far left
MAPLE SUGAR	Definitely a cat's name

MARATHON	A runner's pet
MARBLE	A sculptor's or tileman's pet. Perfect for a calico- or tortoiseshell-colored cat
MARCELLO	An Italian pointer
MARCO	A black and tan coonhound
MARCO POLO	A polo-playing black and tan coonhound
MARDI GRAS	A colorful cat. Perhaps a tortoiseshell
MARGARET	An Abyssinian or a tawny Great Dane
MARIE ANTOINETTE	For a pet with a good head on its shoulders
MARIGOLD	A red Persian or a golden retriever
MARILYN	A very feminine Marilyn Monroe cat
MARINADE	A shaded silver-shaded golden Persian
MARIO	There are several options here—my mechanic or Cuomo are two.
MARIO ANDRETTI	Grand Prix champ. For the racing fan
MARKER	Definitely for a male
MARKS	A dalmatian
MARLO	For someone who watches ''Donahue''
MARLOWE	A detective's pet
MARMALADE	Wonderful cat's name
MARS	For a pet into bars or candy, or acts like it's from outer space
MARSHALL	A law enforcement agent's pet
MARSH-MALLOW	A white, fluffy cat. The white Persian or a Samoyed
MARTHA'S VINEYARD	For the person who wants to be constantly reminded of a peaceful vacation

MARTIN	For a pet with a sheen
MARTY	A butcher's pet from the Bronx
MARVIN	Doesn't this sound like the name of a really loving dog?
MARY	For the pet you can always count on
MARY JANE	A pet into shoes with straps
MARYLOU	A whippet
MARY POPPINS	A bird name, finally
MARZIPAN	A seal point Himalayan, or any sweet pet
MASCOT	A small gray elk dog, or any pet that attends a lot of sporting events
MASH	For those ''M*A*S*H'' diehards
MASON	A Mason Reese or Perry Mason fan's pet, or a bricklayer's pet
MASTER	Any pet that has the upper hand
MATA HARI	A female spy's pet
MATCHMAKER	For the unusual-looking pet you get to walk in the park with you in order to attract attention
MATHERS	For a beaver
MATILDA	For a pet that takes your money and runs to Venezuela. *Everybody!* This is for all you Allan Sherman fans, out there.
MATISSE	A painter's pet
MATTE	A pet whose coat doesn't shine
MATZOH	For a pet that's not quite cooked
MAUD	It always reminds me of Bea Arthur in the seventies show ''Maud.'' A Great Pyrenees would be good.
MAUI	A Hawaiian pet

MAUREEN	For any of the Irish breeds
MAURICE	An Alaskan malamute
MAURY	Would have to be a pair with Connie. An American water spaniel and a Lhasa apso
MAVERICK	Another one of the shows I used to love to watch with my grandmother
MAX	One of the great pet names
MAX HEADROOM	For the taller breeds ... Irish wolfhound, deerhound, borzoi, etcetera
MAXIMILIAN	For any *big* pet, don't you think?
MAXIM'S	The great French restaurant. For any showy female
MAXINE	A Yugoslavian mountain hound. A great female pet name
MAXWELL	Now this is an adorable name. Another one for any pet you like
MAY	For a pet that may or may not be there in the morning
MAYA	A chihuahua
MAYBE	For an indecisive owner
MAYBELLINE	A dog with great skin
MAYBERRY	"The Andy Griffith Show." Is your pet from the South?
MAYDAY	A Saint Bernard!
MAYFLOWER	For a pet that came over from England
MAYHEM	A bichon avanese, or any dog that really needs to be outside
MCALLISTER	A Scottish terrier
MCCLOUD	Another old TV series
MCCOY	For the *real* pet
MCDOOGLE	A Scottish fold

MCDUFF	Ends up being "Duffy." Great for a sheepdog or a police dog
MCENROE	A tennis player's pet
MCGRAW	For an alley cat
MCINTOSH	For any of the Irish breeds, or a pet that loves apples
MCKINLEY	A presidential hopeful's pet
MCMILLAN	The old Rock Hudson TV show, "McMillan and Wife"
MCNALLY	For a map and atlas buff
MCQUEEN	For a butterfly
MEDEA	For a pet that's not too kind to its children
MEDIA	An entertainer's pet
MEDICARE	For the older pet you adopt from the pound
MEDICI	For an Italian pointer from Florence, into banking and the arts
MEDOC	A red Bordeaux wine lover's pet
MEDUSA	For someone with very stringy, curly hair
MEESEKITE	Yiddish for ugliness
MEG	An Australian terrier, about ten inches and 10 pounds, or anyone who's a *Little Women* fan
MEGAN	A Pomeranian ... red fur, lively, cheerful, and barks at strangers
MEL	I love this name for a good-natured male cat or dog
MELBA	Peach. Yummy!

MELBA TOAST	A great nighttime snack. Satisfies the need for chewing something not too fattening
MELLON	A financier's pet
MELLONTOES	Someone's cat is really named that
MELLOW	Great name for a hyperactive pet
MELLY	A chinchilla silver Persian
MELROSE	A pet for someone addicted to evening soaps
MELVILLE	A literary pet
MELVIN	An English bulldog
MEMO	A secretary's pet
MEMPHIS	Elvis Presley fans have an option with this
MENACHEM	A peaceful pet
MENDEL	Austrian monk and botanist 1822–1884. A good name for a scientist's pet
MENTHOL	An ex-smoker's pet
MENU	A chef's pet
MERINGUE	A blue point Birman (which is not blue, but a meringue color)
MERIWETHER	For someone who reads the *Post*
MERLE	European blackbird
MERLIN	A magician's pet
MERMAID	Fish
MERRILL	A cruise line captain's pet
MERRY	The happier version of Mary
MERVIN	A Croatian sheepdog
MESOPOTAMIA	A Turkish van (that's a cat, not a car). Kind of a mouthful, so it works for cats who never come.

METRIC	A displaced European's pet
MEW	A cat sound
MEZZO	For a short pet
MIA	Perfect for a breeding animal . . . lots of babies
MIAMI	For a pet that loves the sun
MIAMI VICE	For a smooth-looking police dog
MICHELANGELO	Italian sculptor, painter, architect, and poet (1475–1564). For the artist's pet
MICHELIN	A "tireless" animal . . . fast on its feet
MICKEY	Good for a mouse . . . pair with Minnie
MICRODOT	Dottie would be the nickname
MICROFILM	Another name for a spy's pet
MICROWAVE	Another good name for the sphinx, because it looks like it came out of a microwave
MIDAS	A rich pet, or any golden-colored pet or breed
MIDAS TOUCH	A pet that will eventually be in commercials
MIDDLEBURY	A well educated animal
MIDNIGHT	This is usually a black animal. We're all so original. . . .
MIDRIFF	Great for a greyhound . . . their ribs stick out a mile.
MIGHTY JOE YOUNG	Any of the big, heavy breeds . . . Newfoundland, Saint Bernard, Bernese mountain dog
MIKADO	An operetta lover's pet
MIKIMOTO	A Japanese bobtail, the best pearl store in the jewelry district

MIKKI	A Chinese crested dog
MILANO	Either a city in Italy or a cookie in America
MILDRED	A redbone coonhound
MILDRED PIERCE	For a Joan Crawford fan
MILFORD	A pet from Connecticut
MILKMAN	Always the one who gets the blame. Good for a cat that comes when the fridge opens
MILLARD	For a pet that's never full ... always wants to fill more
MILLER	An Iceland dog
MILLICENT	Millie's proper name
MILLIE	George and Barbara Bush's dog
MILLSTONE	For any pet that's kind of a burden
MILO	Famous Greek athlete. I think this would be a great pet name. Also pair with Otis
MILQUETOAST	A silver spotted British shorthair. Is your pet timid?
MILTON	A Gordon setter ... I happen to know Milton Gordon. So I like it.
MILTON BERLE	For when your pet is a comedian
MILWAUKEE BRAVE	For a Milwaukee Braves fan's pet, or a fearless pet from Wisconsin
MIMI	This makes me think of a toy poodle
MIMMI	A chow chow
MIMOSA	A type of tree. A type of cocktail
MIMSY	For a pet that gets involved in town gossip
MINERVA	A Manx ... nice name for a cat
MINESTRONE	An Italian hound

MING	For the breeding pet that you expect to start a dynasty
MINIKIN	A darling . . . anything small and rare
MINNA	A Yorkie
MINNESOTA FATS	Jackie Gleason as a basset hound
MINNIE	Mickey Mouse's girlfriend
MINNOW	A Chesapeake Bay retriever, or a fish name for the unoriginal
MINSKOFF	For someone in the theater
MINT JULEP	A American southern long-hair tabby
MINUET	A pet that takes tiny dance steps
MINUTEMAN	A pet that doesn't dawdle when you take it out
MINUTE MOUSE	For the gerbil, mouse, or hamster that you don't expect to last too long
MIRABELLA	Great women's magazine. So good for a pet that likes to leaf through magazines
MIRABELLE	European plum tree (that's a tree, not another animal with a strange name). Poodle? Pomeranian? One of the small dogs
MIRANDA	For a pet not sure of its sexuality
MIRÓ	A painter's pet
MISHA	A ballet dancer's pet
MISS AMERICA	American pit bull terrier . . . no chauvinism here!
MISS BROOKS	A pet you can call "our"
MISS DAISY	A pet that likes to be driven
MISS KITTY	Any adorable kitten . . . who has a sheriff for a boyfriend

MISS LONELYHEARTS	A neutered pet
MISS MARPLE	A pet for an Agatha Christie fan
MISS MONEYPENNY	Pair with James Bond
MISS MUFFET	For any pet that has its own tuffet
MISS PIGGY	For a pig, or a pet that overeats
MISS PRIGGY	Ridiculous
MISS PURRFECT	Also ridiculous, however there are cats out there with that name
MISS VICKY	For a pet that likes to tiptoe through the tulips
MISSHIE	For a Maine coon
MISSILE	For a hyperactive pet
MISSION IMPOSSIBLE	For the absolutely untrainable pet
MISSONI	A designer's pet
MISSY	My ex-husband's cat
MISTER	A former knight's pet
MISTI	A blue Tonkinese
MISTLETOE	For a very affectionate pet
MISTRAL	Frederic, a poet. Also a strong wind in Provence. So, a poet with gas
MISTY	A weatherman's pet
MITCH	An American foxhound . . . sweet and affectionate, but a hard worker
MITCHELL	A Labrador retriever. A good solid name
MITTENS	For any pet that has different color paws
MIZRAHI	A designer's pet
MOBY DICK	For the biggest fish in the tank

MOCHA	A black Oriental shorthair, or any deep brown pet
MODIGLIANI	Artist's pet but a bit of a mouthful
MOE	*See* "Triples," Larry, Curly, and Moe
MOHAWK	A Maremma sheepdog. A wonderful work dog, enemy to the wolf
MOHICAN	For the last of your pets
MOLAR	A dentist's pet
MOLASSES	For a very slow pet
MOLIÈRE	A playwright's pet
MOLLY	One of the more popular names
MOLLY MAGUIRE	For an Irish-American guard dog
MOLOTOV	For the pet that enjoys cocktails
MOMBASA	For a saluki
MONA	For a pet with a wry smile
MONACO	For a royal standard poodle, or a pet into gambling
MONICA	For a cream sphynx . . . a perfect cat name
MONIQUE	For a French pointer
MONOGRAM	For a person whose name is initials, like B.J. or J.B.
MONROE	For a wirehaired pointing griffon
MONTANA	Very cool, western, laid-back name
MONTE CARLO	A gambler's pet
MONTE CRISTO	For a count
MONTESQUIEU	Another regal pet name. Sounds brainy, doesn't it?
MONTGOMERY	For a pet that will live on a cliff(t)
MONTY	For a basset hound

MOOCH	A freeloader's pet
MOODY	Either a Moody Blues fan, or a pet with PMS
MOOKIE	Too cutsie. Although I like Pookie. Go figure
MOOLAH	A rich person's pet
MOON	For a pet with a big face
MOONDOGGIE	Gidget's boyfriend. A surfer's pet
MOON QUEEN	For a blue point Himalayan
MOONSTALK	A cream tabby point Devon rex, or any pet that stays up all night
MOOSE	Either for a Yorkie or a Kuvasz (huge . . . one hundred and ten pounds)
MORDECHAI	For a religious pet
MORGAN	A wonderful sports car. For a pet that wears a belt
MORNING GLORY	An early riser's pet
MORNING STAR	An early riser's pet
MOROCCO	For an exotic pet
MORRIS	A name made famous by the cat food commercial
MORSE CODE	For a pet that, miraculously, knows how to communicate with you
MORTICIA	A mortician's pet . . . pair with Gomez
MORTIMER	A giant schnauzer
MORTON	For an old, salty dog
MOSAIC	For a pet of many colors
MOSCOW	For a borzoi or Russian wolfhound
MOTHER GOOSE	For any breeding animal

MOTOROLA	A pet for a person with a car phone
MOUSER	A mouse chaser's name
MOVADO	For a pet that tells time
MOVER	A good name for a hamster that has a running wheel in its cage
MOXIE	A pushy person's pet
MOZART	A music aficionado's pet
MR. BECKS	A beer lover's pet
MR. BLUE	A depressive's pet
MR. CLEAN	For a pet with an earring
MR. DEEDS	For a pet that goes to town
MR. DOOLEY	For a pet who hangs down his head
MR. MAGOO	For a pug
MR. MEPHISTOFELES	*Cats!*
MR. PEEPERS	Pugs, bulldogs
MR. PRESIDENT	A homeless person's pet
MR. PURRFECT	*See* Miss Purrfect
MR. ROBERTS	A sailor's pet
MR. ROGERS	For a neutered pet
MR. SMITH	For a pet that goes to Washington
MR. T	A bejeweled rough-coated Bohemian pointer
MRS. COLUMBO	For a female version of the scruffy ''Columbo''
MRS. FLETCHER	A mystery writer's pet
MRS. HOWELL	For a ''Gilligan's Island'' fan
MRS. POLIFAX	Wonderful older woman who spies for the CIA
MUCH ADO	For a pet with a flourish

MUELLER	A German hunting terrier
MUFFIE	Muffie reminds me of fluffy, so I would use this for a ragdoll or Persian
MUFFIN	A WASP's pet
MUFFLES	A hard-of-hearing person's pet
MUGGS	For a mixed breed
MUHAMMAD ALI	The great Cassius Clay. It would have to be a boxer.
MULDOON	Toody's partner ... *Car 54, Where Are You?*
MULLIGAN STEW	For a mixed breed
MUMBLES	Good name for a parrot
MUMMY	A rap person's pet. (Get it? Wrapped? *The Mummy*?)
MUMPS	For a pug or a bulldog
MUPPET	For a pet that looks like a puppet
MURIEL	Another perfect animal name
MURPHY	Irish wolfhound, Irish setter, Irish terrier, etcetera
MURPHY BROWN	A reporter's pet
MURRAY	One of those names that is outstanding for any animal, also good for the "Mad About You" fan
MUSCLES	For a boxer
MUSHROOM	For the pet that will get much bigger than you originally thought
MUSTARD	For a golden Persian, or any golden colored pets
MUTZIE	For a female mixed breed
MUUMUU	A fat person's pet

MY FRIEND FLICKA	For your horse
MYLAR	For a silver pointed tabby, or any silver-furred pet
MY MAN GODFREY	Great movie, and Godfrey is a wonderful pet name
MYTH	Perfect for someone with a lithp
MYTHTER	Also great for someone with a lithp.

NABBER	For a mouser
NABOKOV	Vladimir ... any Russian or literary pet
NABOR	For your neighbor named Jim, or a pet with a deep singing voice
NADER	Activist pet ... demands constant consumer protection
NAGGER	A pet that doesn't stop whining till you feed it
NAIAD	Myth. A nymph of a lake, river, etcetera
NAMATH	For a pet that loves football or has bad knees
NAMELESS	When, try as you might, you just can't come up with a name
NAMO	One of Charlemagne's knights
NANA	The Newfoundland from *Peter Pan*
NANCY	I can't imagine a cuter name for a pet
NANCY DREW	For a pet of mysterious parentage
NANNY	Another one for the Newfoundland
NANTERS	Myth. British king
NANTES	Myth. Site of Caradoc's castle

NANTUCKET	For a pet you have to get to by ferry
NAPA	For a wine loving pet from the valley
NAPE	Another name from mythology. One of the dogs pursuing Actaeon after Diana changed him into a stag.
NAPOLEON	For a Yorkie. Is your pet the leader of the pack?
NARCISSUS	Is your pet vain?
NARNIA	For a cavalier King Charles Spaniel. For someone who loves *The Chronicles of Narnia*
NARRATOR	Another good parrot name
NASH	For an Ogden
NASHUA	A pet from a New Hampshire industrial town
NASHVILLE	For a country western lover's pet
NASSER	For a high ranking Egyptian official's pet
NASSIM	A Russian name
NASTASE	Sounds Russian, but it's definitely tennis
NAT	Seems like a very chummy name for your pet
NATALIE	I don't want to say woodpecker, so I will say a smooth fox terrier
NATASHA	A Russian wolfhound
NATE	Al's partner in the L.A. Deli
NATIONAL	An aspiring Budget rental agent's pet
NATIONAL VELVET	Elizabeth Taylor's horse story
NATIVE SON	For an all-American pet
NATURAL	For a puli
NATWICK	A pet for a Mildred

NAUSICAA	From Homer . . . daughter of Alcinous
NAUSITHOUS	Myth. King of the Phaeacians
NAVAJO	*See* Native Son
NAVARRO	Prefers to go by airplane instead
NAVEL	An orange pet
NAVRATILOVA	A tennis player's pet
NAVY	A sailor's pet
NAXOS	Largest island of the Cyclades in the Aegean Sea
NBC	*See* "Triples," CBS, ABC, and NBC
NEAL	Wouldn't this be terrific for a big goofy dog?
NEBUCHAD-NEZZAR	A mean Old Testament King
NECK	For a bulldog
NECTAR	Celestial beverage of the gods
NED	A Beatty pet
NEGOTIATOR	For the pet that makes peace in the family
NEGRI	For a black cat
NEGUS	An Amharic word meaning "king"
NEHRU	For an Indian cat
NEIMAN	A shopper's pet. Pair with Marcus
NELLIA	For a tortie lilac lynx point Siamese
NELLIE	For a tortie seal lynx point Siamese
NELLY	This ranks right up there with Molly for great pet names
NELLYBELLE	Roy Rogers' Jeep
NELSON	For an "Ozzie and Harriet" fan

NEMEA	Myth. Nemean games were held in honor of Jupiter and Hercules
NEMESIS	Goddess of just retribution
NENNI	For a seal bicolor ragdoll
NEON	For a flashy pet
NEOPTOLEMUS	Son of Achilles
NEOSHO	Japanese beetle
NEPENTHE	Myth. Egyptian drug fabled to drive away cares and woes
NEPHELE	Myth. Mother of Phyrius and Helle
NEPHTHYS	Myth. Egyptian Goddess
NEPTUNE	For one of the larger fish in the tank
NEREIDS	Myth. Sea nymphs . . . daughters of Nereus and Doris. A good group name for a tank of fish
NEREUS	Myth. Father of the water nymphs. For any pet that loves to swim
NERO	Fiddle-playing pet
NESBITT	A pet for a Cathleen
NESSUS	Myth. Centaur killed by Hercules
NESTOR	Myth. King of Pylos, renowned for his wisdom
NETTLA	A character from Bambi
NETWORK	An aspiring cable executive's pet
NEURON	For a very small pet
NEVADA	A quickie divorced person's pet
NEVIL	For a Gordon setter . . . Scottish ancestry, intelligent and pleasant
NEWBURY	For someone who likes Boston
NEW JERSEY	For someone who moved from
NEWLEY	For an Anthony

NEWMAN	For a Paul
NEWPORT	For a Californian
NEWS ITEM	Perfect for a parrot
NEWSWEEK	For a pet that likes to keep on top of current events
NEWTON	For a Sir Isaac, or a pet that likes juice
NEW YEAR'S	For a very festive pet
THE NEW YORKER	For a pet from New York, living elsewhere
NEXT	For the second of a litter
NFL	A Sunday football widow's pet
NIAGARA	Dogs partial to wearing highly starched collars, or a pet with a big bladder
NIBBLER	For a gerbil
NIBELUNG	Myth. Originally a race of dwarfs ... is your pet small? Another good fish tank name
NICCOLO	That commercial drives me crazy, but if *you* want to keep yelling, "N i c c o l o!" go ahead
NICHOLAS	Good name. My friend's Jack Russell terrier in New Hampshire has this name
NICHOLAS NICKELBY	Perfect for a Dickens fan
NICHOLS	For someone who likes to shop in London
NICK	Asta's pet (*see* Nora). We know who *really* solved those mysteries.
NICK AT NIGHT	For an outdoor guard dog
NICK CHARLES	Nora Charles' husband in *The Thin Man* series

NICKELODEON	For an active TV family
NICKIE	What Nora called Nick in *The Thin Man* series
NICKS	What Nora *was* in *The Thin Man* series
NICOLAI	Russian wolfhound
NICOLE	For a chestnut Angora
NICOLET	French bulldog
NICOLETTE	For a little French poodle
NIDIA	Not quite a Lidia
NIETZSCHE	For a very philosophical pet
NIFLHEIM	Myth. One of the nine worlds
NIFTY	A cool pet
NIGEL	Great! A giant schnauzer, Saint Bernard, Great Dane, etcetera
NIGGS	A teeny-weeny silky terrier
NIGHT	Any black animal
NIGHTINGALE	A nurse's pet
NIJINSKY	A dancer's pet
NIKE	For a greyhound or any pet that's fast
NIKITA	For a Russian borzoi
NIKKI	The borzoi's nickname
NILE	For a river animal
NILES	Frasier's brother. I can see this for a dog.
NIM	Kim's brother
NIMBUS	For a cloudy pet
NIMITZ	For a black and white smoke Devon rex. Is your pet an admiral?
NIMOY	For a pet that has pointy ears
NIMROD	A mighty hunter ... grandson of Noah and descendant of Ham

NIN	For an Anaïs fan
NIÑA	Triple with Pinta and Santa Maria
NINE	For a daring cat
NINETY-NINE	Maxwell Smart's partner
NINI	For an Italian pointer
NINNIUS	Myth. Brother of Cassibellaun, conquered by Caesar
NINO	For a volpino Italiano ... this dog stays under nine pounds
NINTENDO	For a pet that keeps your kids company for hours at the TV
NINUS	Myth. Son of Belus and reputed builder of Nineveh
NIOBE	Myth. Daughter of Tantalus and queen of Thebes
NIPPER	The little nipper (better than a big nipper)
NISUS	Myth. A king of Megara ... he was changed into an eagle. Finally, another bird name
NITA	A very clean pet
NITDHOGG	Myth. A serpent ... so there's a good one for snakes
NIVEN	A pet for a David
NIVIE	For a smooth fox terrier
NIVINS	Sounds like a butler
NIXON	*See* Checkers
NOAH	An ark builder's pet
NOAM	For a miniature Alaskan husky (malamute)
NOBEL	For a show dog ... usually wins the blue ribbon
NOBLEMAN	For a Spanish mastiff

NOEL	For a pet born on Christmas day
NOGUCHI	A sculptor's pet
NOISE	For a pet that won't stop talking, barking, mewing, or whatever
NOLTE	For a Nick fan
NOMAD	For an alley cat
NONCHALANT	For a very mellow and casual pet
NONPARTISAN	An independent's pet
NOODLES	For a pasta fan
NORA	*See* Nick
NORA CHARLES	Nick Charles' wife in *The Thin Man* series
NORBERT	Nor Ernie, either
NORBIE	For a bichon frise
NOREEN	For an Irish setter, Irish wolfhound, Irish terrier, etcetera
NOREL	For an Australian silky terrier
NORELL	For the perfume lover
NORM	''Cheers'' anyone?
NORMA	My aunt
NORRIS	Chuck anyone?
NORSEMAN	Norwegian elkhound
NORTH	This one's for Ollie
NORTH POLE	For a Siberian husky
NORTON	Kramden's pal
NORVELL	For a border terrier
NORWAY	For a Norwegian elkhound
NORWOOD	For an American foxhound
NOSTALGIA	A cat on its ninth life . . . wants to be back in one of the previous eight
NOSTRADAMUS	For a stargazer

NOTEWORTHY	For a pet that one notices
NOTHUNG	Myth. A magic sword
NOTORIOUS	For a Hitchcock fan
NOTUS	Myth. Personification of the south wind ... good for a bird
NOVAK	For a Kim or a Siamese
NOVA SCOTIA	For your not too salty fish
NOVELLA	An author's pet
NOVEMBER	For a pet you get in November
NOW	National Organization of Women ... a feminist's pet
NOX	Myth. A goddess
NOXZEMA	For a very clean pet with good skin
NUFFI	For a Newfoundland
NUKE	Bionic dog
NUMA POMPILIUS	Legendary second king of Rome
NUMBERS	A gambler's pet
NUNZIE	For a ruddy wild Abyssinian
NUNZIO	For an Italian greyhound
NUPTIAL	For a pet that's a wedding gift
NUREYEV	A dancer's pet
NURSE RATCHET	For a nasty ole cat ready to fly over the cuckoo's nest
NUTMEG	A pet named Meg that's a little out to lunch
NYET	Needs obedience school
NYMPH	For one of your smaller breeds
NYMPHET	For an even smaller breed, light on its feet
NYNEX	When your phone bill is consistently higher than your mortgage

O.J.	I guess this is a no-no right now
OAKIE	Remember "Oakie Fanoakie"? It's a cute name if you think about it.
OAKLAND	A pet from California
OAKLEY	An Annie fan
OASIS	For a pet from the desert
OATCAKE	For someone on a diet
OATES	Great name. Sounds just right when you say it
OATH	A judge's pet
OATIE	Oatmeal's nickname
OATMEAL	For someone who likes a hearty breakfast
OATS	For a silky terrier ... lively and cheerful ... can really feel its oats
OATSUNG	The actual pronunciation of Oudtshoorn (*see* following)
OBERARTH	A small Swiss village. For a pet that likes the Alps
OBERRUNON	Also a small Swiss village, where I lived for one month ... too long
OBERTH	For a brood mare

OBI	Wan Kenobi ... for a *Star Wars* fan
OBIE	For a bloodhound .. wonderful sense of smell, timid, and good-natured
OBLONG	For a wirehaired dachshund
O'BRIEN	For an Irish wolfhound
O'CASEY	For an Irish setter
OCEAN	Fish or a whole fish tank
OCEANUS	Myth. A Titan ruling the watery elements
O'CONNOR	For an "All in the Family" fan
OCTOBER	A pet born in October
OCYRRHOE	Myth. A prophetess
ODALIS	For a basset griffon vendéen ... small but courageous and tenacious
ODDJOB	A pet that can toss a hat and make an impact
ODELIA	For a King Charles spaniel
ODERIC	Myth. The false night
ODESSA	For someone who likes filing
ODETTA	Are you into folk music?
ODIE	For a great Swiss mountain dog ... loyal, courageous, and wise
ODIN	Myth. God of wisdom. The supreme god of Norse mythology. Does your Great Dane rule your home?
ODYAR	A famous Frankis hero
ODYSSEUS	For a borzoi
ODYSSEY	Homer's poem
ODYSSIA	For a bronze Egyptian mau
OEDIPUP	A puppy with an oeidpal complex
OEDIPUSS	A kitty with an oeidpal complex

OEDIPUS REX	The king of all oedipal complexes
OENEUS	Myth. A king of Calydon
OENONE	Myth. A nymph married by Paris in his youth
OENOPION	Myth. King of Chios
OETA	Myth. Scene of Hercules' death
OFFBEAT	A pet without an oedipal complex
OFFICER	For a guard dog
OGIER THE DANE	One of the great heroes of medieval romance
O'HARA	For a Scarlett pet, or a southern one
OHIO	For a Japanese spitz
OHRBACH	For a nostalgic shopper
OKALOOSA	Sounds like a basset hound
O'KEEFE	For a white Manx
O'KEEFFE	A pet from Georgia, or a pet into strange-looking flowers
OKEMO	A Rhodesian ridgeback
OKTOBERFEST	For a pet that loves beer
OLAF	A Bosnian hound
OLD ENGLISH	A great aftershave . . . a pet that smells good
OLD FAITHFUL	Good for a Labrador . . . reminds me of Old Yeller
OLD MAID	For a female that's never had a litter
OLD MAN	For a male that's too old to have a litter
OLD MAN AND THE SEA	For an old Portuguese water dog and his fish
OLD YELLER	A yellow Labrador retriever
OLÉ	For a bull

OLEANDER	For a golden Persian
O'LEARY	For an Irish pet that's a bit on the cautious side
OLIVE OYL	For either a Popeye fan, or a salad lover
OLIVER	For a pet with a love story
OLIVER TWIST	For a pet you rescue from the pound
OLIVIA	An actor's pet
OLIVIER	Also an actor's pet
OLLIE	Also an actor's pet
OLLY	Triple with Kookla and Fran
OLSEN	Lois Lane's coworker, Jimmy
OLWEN	Myth. Wife of Kilwich
OLYMPIA	Myth. A valley in Elis, celebrated for the sanctuary of Zeus
OLYMPIAN	For a harlequin Great Dane
OLYMPIAN ZEUS	A Great Dane
OLYMPUS	Dwelling place of the dynasty of gods
OMAR	For an Egyptian sphynx
OMAR KHAYYÁM	Eleventh-century Persian poet
OMBUDSMAN	For the pet that you appoint to investigate complaints within the family
OMEGA	A watcher, or the last pet you think you'll own. Pair with Alpha
OMELET	A French mastiff, or any pet that likes eggs
OMPHALE	Myth. Queen of Lydia to whom Hercules was bound as a slave and then fell in love with
ONASSIS	For a Greek hound

ONCE	For a pet that listens and obeys the first time
ONDREI	For a small continental spaniel
ONEIDA	For someone into silverware
O'NEILL	For a pet in the theater
ONION	For a pet with a lot of layers
ONO	For a naughty pet
ONOMATOPOEIA	For a pet with good grammar
ONYX	For a black smoke American shorthair
OODLES OF NOODLES	For a Cairn terrier . . . lively and lovable
OOH	For a bull terrier
OOPLA	For a pet that likes being thrown up in the air—and caught
OPAL	For a blue-cream point Himalayan
OPAQUE	For a pet that you can't see through
OPERA	An opera lover's pet
OPERATOR	The neighborhood gossip
OPHELLIA	For an Afghan
OPHION	Myth. The king of the Titans
OPIE	''The Andy Griffith Show''
OPPENHEIMER	For a pet that's into investing
OPRAH	For a talkative pet
OPTION	A stockbroker's pet
OPUS	A great work of writing or music. Another best of breed name
ORANGE	For a plain, old orange and white tabby
ORANGEADE	For a red spotted British shorthair
ORANGE BLOSSOM	For a red Oriental shorthair

ORANGE JULIUS	For a red Oriental shorthair
ORANTES	For an athletic pet
ORBIS	For a fish
ORBIT	For a bird
ORC	Myth. A sea monster that devoured men and women
ORCHID	For a very delicate pet that needs constant room temperature
OREAD	Myth. A mountain or hill nymph
O'REE	For an Irish blue terrier
OREGANO	For an Italian hound
OREO	For a black and white anything
ORESTES	Myth. Son of Agamemnon and Clytemnestra
ORGANDY	For a beautiful, fluffy, willowy cat
ORGANZA	For a rather stiff but still feminine cat
ORIGINAL SIN	For a snake
ORION	Myth. A giant and hunter, son of Neptune. Eventually placed as a constellation with dog Sirius following him
ORITHYIA	Myth. A nymph
ORLANDO	For someone who loves Disney World, or nephew of Charlemagne, celebrated knight
ORLOFF	For a black smoke and white Scottish fold
ORMANDY	A conductor's pet
ORNAMENT	What my friend told her husband she was when he asked her to get a job. A good name for a lap dog
ORNATE	For an ultrafancy pet
O'ROURKE	For an Irish water spaniel

ORPHA	For a Dandie Dinmont terrier
ORPHEE	For an akita
ORPHEUS	Myth. Son of Apollo and Calliope
ORTEGA	For a Spanish mastiff . . . big, robust guard dog, but vivacious and affectionate
ORTHODOX	For a religious pet
ORVIS	For an athletic pet
ORWELL	For a pet born in 1984
O'RYAN	A movie lover's pet
ORZO	For a pasta-loving pet
OSBORNE	For an American foxhound
OSCAR	For a pet that loves the trash and is always grouchy
OSGOOD	For a pet into bow ties
OSHA	For a government pet
O'SHEA	For an Irish terrier
OSHKOSH	For a pet into overalls
OSIRIS	One of the chief gods of Egyptian mythology
OSKAR	For a German shepherd
OSLO	For a Swedish Elkhound
OSMOND	For a Donny or Marie
OSMOSIS	For a pet that does your bidding without your saying a word
OSSA	Myth. Mountain in Thessaly
OSSI	For an ossicat
OSSIAN	Legendary Gaelic bard and warrior of the third century
OSSIP	For someone who's not quite a gossip
OSTENTATIOUS	For a flashy pet

O'SULLIVAN	For a pet with a famous daughter … Maureen and Mia
OSWALD	For a pit bull that acts alone
OTHELLO	For a Shakespeare buff
OTIS	Wonderful pet name. Appropriate for almost any type of animal or breed
OTIS REDDING	For a pet that likes to sit in the mornin' sun
O'TOOLE	A Peter fan
OTTO	This is also one of those universal, endearing names
OUDTSHOORN	A town in South Africa where they breed ostriches (*see* Oatsung)
OUNCE	For your smaller breeds
OUTDO	For a pet that's going to be wearing great collars
OUTIE	Innie's brother
OUTLAW	Any pet that has dark rings around both eyes
OUTLET	A shopper's pet
OUTRAGEOUS	Not for a meek pet
OUTSIDER	For an outdoor pet
OUTTAKE	A TV producer's pet
OVID	Latin poet in the time of Augustus
OWAIN	A knight of King Arthur's court
OWEN	Marshall … counselor at law
OWNER	Just who's the boss?
OXFORD	For someone into good sheets
OZ	For a wizard
OZANNA	A knight of King Arthur's round table
OZAWA	A Rhodesian ridgeback

OZER   For a funny-looking pet

OZONE   For a pet with its head in the clouds

OZZIE   Harriet, Ricky, and David ... the Nelson family

PABLO   Any of the Spanish breeds ... Spanish mastiff, Spanish greyhound, etcetera

PACKER   A pet that's always threatening to leave

PADDY   Irish wolfhound, Irish setter, Irish water dog

PAIGE   A fifties WASPish name that doesn't seem to be so popular any more, at least not with pets

PAISLEY   A pet with a lot of colors, tortoise-shell and white American wirehair, for instance

PALADIN   The wonderful gunslinging cowboy from the sixties TV show

PALAHVI   Where caviar is harvested ... for something in your fish tank

PALERMO   A Sicilian pet

PALM BEACH   Sunny and rich. An Afghan would be gorgeous.

PALOMA   The famous Pablo Picasso's daughter ... this also makes me think of Afghans

PAM	Perfect for a brown classic tabby American shorthair
PAMELA	Pam's given name
PANACEA	You can't believe it's so perfect
PANACHE	A dog with style and flair
PANAMA	A pet into hats
PANDORA	A pet constantly coming up with unpleasant surprises
PANSY	Triple with Rose and Violet
PAOLO	Portuguese water dog, Spanish mastiff, Chihuahua
PAR	A golfer's pet
PARADISE	An American pet that is just perfect in every way
PARADISO	An Italian pet that is just perfect in every way
PARALLAX	A pet that gives you a different view
PARIS	It was the last time you saw it
PARKAY	When it looks so good, you can't believe that it's not purebred
PARKER	For someone who loves pens
PARKWAY	For those who don't live near highways
PARMESAN	Not what I would call a cheesy name ... I think it's great
PARSLEY	The green vegetable that is good for bad breath
PARTNER	A pet that goes to work with you
PARTRIDGE	For a pet with a large family
PARTY GIRL	A Scottish fold, or any outgoing female pet
PARVIS	Part this, and part that ... for a mutt

PASCAL	For a Bedlington terrier (it looks like a lamb)
PASHA	For any of the royal breeds ... King Charles spaniel, royal standard poodle, etcetera
PASSION	Great for a pit bull
PASTA	My son's favorite food in the entire world
PASTERNAK	For a *Dr. Zhivago* fan
PASTEUR	A dairyman's pet
PATCHWORK	A pet of many colors
PATEK	Any of the French breeds
PATEK PHILIPPE	Any of the French breeds that watch the time
PATHFINDER	Any of the hunting breeds
PATRICK	For any of the Irish breeds ... setters, Irish terriers, Irish wolfhounds, etcetera
PATRICK HENRY	For any of the Irish breeds that were born in America
PATRIOT	Any pet that stands at attention when the national anthem is played
PATSY	For the pet that always takes the blame
PATTON	For the pet that should take the blame
PAUL BUNYAN	Either for your giant breeds, or for a Paul with problem feet
PAVAROTTI	A pet with huge lungs
PAVÉ	A pet for someone in the diamond business
PAVLOV	You think he's trained, but *you're* the one going out as soon as you wake up

PAVLOVA	Russian ballerina . . . borzoi, tall and graceful
PAWS	Nice name for a cat with different color paws
PAX	For a peaceful pet
PAYOLA	Perfect for a disc jockey from the sixties
PEABODY	English bulldog, English foxhound, English setter
PEACHES	Pair with Cream
PEANUT	For any of your toy breeds
PEANUT BUTTER	Pair with jelly. By the way, it's good for getting chewing gum out of hair. I don't know about fur.
PEAR	A fruit lover's pet
PEARL	For any of your mini's
PEA SHOOTER	Good for a rabbit
PEAT	A gardener's pet
PEBBLES	Pair with Bamm Bamm
PECK	For an affectionate pet
PEDRO	Would make a cute name for a French or Old English bulldog
PEEPERS	A nearsighted animal. Good for an Old English sheepdog
PEGASUS	Finally, a name for a horse! Hopefully, it didn't spring from Medusa's body upon her death.
PEGGY	For an honest-to-goodness, easygoing, reliable pet
PÉLÉ	For a pet that's good with its feet
PEN	An ex-con's pet
PENDLETON	For a briard, bearded collie, brindle Great Dane

PENELOPE	For a pet that costs more than a penny
PENNE	Another type of pasta
PENNY	A pet that cost less than Penelope
PENROD	A wirehaired dachshund
PEONY	Wonderful in an arrangement with Blossom, Violet, Daisy, and Daffodil
PEORIA	For someone from Illinois
PEPA	Pair with Salt
PEPPER	Pair with Salt (and that's it for Salt pairs)
PEPPERMINT	For your fresh smelling pet
PEPPERONI	For your spotted pets
PEPPY	What a name for a basset hound
PEPSI	Pair with Coke
PERCY	Percy Sledge, or any pet that's into poetry
PERIWINKLE	A snail or mussel, or any of your blue breeds
PERKINS	For a pet that would make a terrific butler
PERÓN	For a dictatorial pet
PEROT	Wants to run for office
PEROXIDE	A blonde's pet (I'm sorry, I couldn't resist)
PERRY	Great for Perry Mason fans. Female pairing would be Della
PERSIA	A Persian . . . what else?
PERSNICKETY	For a fastidious, fussy pet
PESKY	The original name for mosquitoes
PESTO	Gooey green sauce, full of garlic. Good for a skunk

PETE	Good, solid work dog
PETER	Pete's formal name
PETER PAN	For a pet that refuses to grow up
PETIT FOUR	For a yummy, many layered, multi-faceted cat
PETRA	For a formal type of animal
PETUNIA	Yet another flower
PHANTOM	Good name for a disappearing cat
PHARAOH	The pharaoh hound. That was easy.
PHI BETA KAPPA	You didn't make it, but hope your pet will make up for it
PHILADELPHIA	For a Grace Kelly fan, or for a pet that's full of brotherly love
PHILIE	A whipped Philip
PHILIP	A queen's Philip
PHILIP MORRIS	A smoker's pet
PHILIPPA	Female Philip
PHILIPPE	French Philip
PHINEAS	A Scottish terrier
PHOEBE	Another of the great pet names . . . good for any type of female
PHOENICIA	For an exotic, long-haired pet
PHOENIX	For any pet that rises again and again
PHONOGRAPH	For the old-timers who remember the days before tapes, CDs, CD ROMs, video, audio, stereo, and all the rest of that stuff
PHYLLIS	Phyllis Diller: queen of comedy, piano, and plastic surgery
PHYLLO DOUGH	For a Greek hound that enjoys a good pastry now and then

PIA Another pet that has questionable control skills

PIAF For aficionados of cabaret singers

PIANO A mitted tabby that walks the piano keys

PICA For a very small breed, reminiscent of small print

PICASSO An artist's pet

PICAYUNE An accountant's pet, or for a small breed

PICCADILLY For those who love London

PICCOLO It means "small" in Italian. So, perhaps a good name for a small Italian animal

PICKETT For a sign-carrying pet, or a Wilson Pickett fan

PICKLES For the pet that leaves a sour taste in your mouth

PICKWICK For a pet that goes on papers

PIED PIPER A pet in heat

PIERRE How very French, my dear. A standard poodle, French bulldog

PIKE For a very tall breed, reminiscent of Pike's Peak

PILAR For a pet from India

PILOT I know there's a type of dog featured with goggles on, behind the wheel of a plane

PILS A beer lover's pet

PIM Blue Abyssinian, silver spotted British shorthair, or California spangled

PINKERTON For any of the English detective-type breeds

PINK LADY	I remember having this drink in high school, but, I don't remember what it was. A French poodle with a fancy haircut
PINKNEY	My vet, and a good name
PINK PANTHER	For a pet that constantly sneaks up on you
PINKY	Chihuahua or pig
PINKY LEE	Television star and show of the same name
PINOCCHIO	Any pet with a long snout . . . a dachshund would be perfect
PINTO BEAN	Also for a Chihuahua (I will *never* learn to spell this without looking it up)
PIONEER	A pet for someone in the electronics business
PIP	For a pet that can take a joke
PIPER	Piper Laurie
PIPPI	Pippi Longstocking
PIPPIN	They named a Broadway show after it
PIP-SQUEAK	Pip's full name
PIRATE	Any pet that steals your food or clothing
PI SQUARED	A mathematician's pet
PISSARRO	Camille . . . Impressionist
PISTACHIO	So good, but so much work
PITA	For a kangaroo
PITTER	Patter's playmate
PIXIE	For a silky terrier or any of your smaller breeds, or a Doberman

PIZARRO	Francisco (1475–1541), Spanish conqueror of Peru. May be good for a Portuguese water dog
PIZZA	A restaurateur's pet
PIZZAZZ	An animal with real style and charm
PJ	A cat that loves to sleep
PLACEBO	For people who have bought a pet because they are not ready to have kids yet
PLANET HOLLYWOOD	For a pet that loves the limelight
PLASTIC	For *The Graduate*
PLATH	For a depressed pet
PLATO	A very studious pet, or a pet that knows when to retreat
PLATOON	An English bulldog
PLAYBOY	For an unneutered male
PLAYER	A Jack Russell terrier that keeps bringing the damn ball back over and over and over and over
PLAZA	Ivana Trump's former pet. Are you into luxury hotels?
PLUM	The pick of the litter
PLUTO	Disney cartoon character
PMS	For the pet that is occassionally moody with a tendency to bite
POACHER	Any animal that likes to steal food
POE	As in Edgar Allan
POET	An English bulldog wearing glasses
POGO	Reminds me of a Dandie Dinmont terrier
POINSETTIA	Any showy animal

POINTER	Not very original, but a good name for a German shorthaired pointer
POLARIS	The North Star, or the U.S. ballistic missile with a nuclear warhead. So either a sweet and cuddly pet or a lunatic
POLAR STAR	An outdoor pet
POLICY	A congressman's pet
POLIFAX	For those into the Mrs. Polifax mysteries
POLLY	I know "Polly wanna cracker" is pushing it, but hey, this isn't so easy!
POLO	For a Ralph or a Marco
POLYGAMIST	A stud animal
POMPIDOU	French bulldog
POM POM	My favorite movie candy when I was young. They are now called Milk Duds.
PONCE DE LEÓN	You live in Florida and believe that this pet is the answer
PONCHO	Great for a chihuahua
POOCHI	A doggie designer
POOCHINI	A doggie composer
POODIE	For a peekapoo (poodle and Pekingese combination)
POOF	What happens to "Puddles" if he doesn't shape up quickly! (*see* Puddles)
POOH BAH	From Gilbert and Sullivan's *The Mikado*.
POOH BEAR	From *Winnie the Pooh*
POOR RICHARD	For the cat you get while still owning three dogs

POPCORN   Great for a bichon avanese, or any fluffy white pet

POPPER   A Japanese bobtail

POPPY   For the stud animal

PORGY   Pair with Bess

PORSCHE   One day I will get this ... a 1957 would make me so happy, not to mention so poor. A great name for a greyhound

PORT   A lovely wine that's a bit heavy.

PORTABLE   A Yorkie or a silky terrier

PORTER   A pet either good with luggage, or good with music

PORTFOLIO   An investment banker's pet

PORTIA   The heroine in Shakespeare's *Merchant of Venice*

PORTNOY   For the pet that never stops complaining

PORTOBELLO   For a pet that likes mushrooms

POSTCARD   For a traveling man

POSTMAN   When you're not sure who the father was

POT   Pair with Pan

POTLUCK   What you see is what you get

POTPIE   A fat little cat! Cream and white Persian

POTTER   Colonel Potter from ''M*A*S*H.'' For the ''M*A*S*H'' fan

POTTS   Different from ''pots and pans'' ... an English pet, perhaps

POUNCE   A cat that loves to jump

POWDER   Possibility for those interested in the white stuff ... snow

PRADA

For a very expensive pet of Italian heritage

PRANCER

If you have a reindeer . . . perfection

PREAKNESS

For a racing aficionado

PRECIOUS

Usually a nickname

PREDATOR

Good name for either a Doberman or a Yorkie

PREEMIE

Perfect for a sphynx. They are hairless and wrinkled and always look like they were just born.

PREPPIE

American shorthair

PRESLEY

For an Elvis fan

PRESSROOM

A very busy animal

PRESTO

A Devon rex (hairless)

PRESTON

A collie (they can't all be Lassie)

PRETTY WOMAN

You like both the song and the movie

PRETZEL

For an animal that turns you inside out

PRIAM

Last king of Troy during the Trojan War

PRIDE

You've decided to get a pet instead of a kid

PRIMA BALLERINA

An exotic shorthair

PRIMO

The best

PRIMROSE

Another flower. Do you remember the song "Primrose Lane" by Pat Boone?

PRINCE

Once every girl's dream . . . to marry a prince and ride off into the sunset

PRINCE CHARMING

Cinderella's knight in shining armor

PRINCE CHARLES	Cinderella's ex-knight in shining armor
PRINCE OF TIDES	Barbra Streisand's wanna be knight in shining armor
PRINCESS	Once upon a time a beautiful dream . . . today a can of worms
PRINCESS DI	Just ask her!
PRINCE VALIANT	The prince no one's seemed to find yet
PRINTER	A pet that makes an impression
PRINTOUT	Mynah birds, parrots
PRISCILLA	I once baby-sat for Priscilla Poodle, a mini that was simply charming. Or, it's another choice for Elvis fans.
PRISSIE	Nickname for Priscilla
PRO	Nickname for a pet on the show circuit
PROFESSOR	For a very smart pet
PROKOFIEV	Russian composer, Sergey. A borzoi would be wonderful
PROM	You went, loved it, and don't want to forget it
PROMETHEUS	Something about fire for mankind and vultures eating his liver as punishment. Heavy stuff for a small pet
PROOF	An alcoholic's pet
PROUST	Either a literary pet or one that dances
PROWLER	A cat or dog with dark circles around its eyes
PRUDENCE	A pet you bought carefully
PRUNELLA	Pugs, bulldogs, boxers
PSYCHO	You'll know if it fits

PUCCI	Designer still in business after all these years . . . same weird color combinations
PUCCINI	Classical composer, a.k.a. Giacomo. Famous for operas . . . any "pooch" will do
PUCK	A hockey fan's pet
PUDDING	There seems to be a run on "Pudding" for Yorkshire terriers
PUDDLES	A dog that has been having problems with housebreaking
PUDGY	The nickname of a boy in my class. We never thought twice about it. I wonder if he did.
PUFF	For a magic dragon
PUIFORCAT	For a very sweet, dessertish cat
PULITZER	A prizewinning pet
PUMPERNICKEL	For any of your dark brown to black pets
PUMPKIN	An orange and black tabby, or an American wirehair
PUNCH	Pair with Judy
PUNKY	"Punky Brewster," a TV show . . . all grown up now
PUREE	A cook's pet
PURPLE PASSION	A dog or cat that drives one to such lengths that the purple vein in your neck sticks out!
PURRFECT	For the perfect cat
PURRFECTLY	Too syrupy
PURRY FURR	A winner at the Madison Square Garden Cat Show
PUSHKIN	Pugs, bulldogs, boxers

PUSS-IN-BOOTS   What else but a rat with "mittens"

PUSSYWILLOW   Perfect for any cat

PUTTER   A golfer's pet

PUZO   For a pet with a godfather

PYEWACKET   The cat from *Bell, Book & Candle*

PYGMALION   For a pet you got from the pound that turned out to have a pedigree

QANTAS	For an Airedale
QUACK	A doctor's pet
QUAID	A Dennis or Randy fan
QUAINT	For a nice, old-fashioned pet
QUAKER	A gentle pet
QUANTUM LEAP	For a time traveler
QUARANTINE	For a pet that's always sick
QUARK	A very, very tiny pet
QUARTERBACK	For someone always barking orders
QUARTZ	Takes a licking and keeps on ticking
QUASI	Almost
QUASIMODO	Turtles, Shar-peis, pugs, bulldogs, reptiles
QUAYLE	For the potato lover's pet
QUEASY	For the pet that's partial to Alka-Seltzer
QUEEN	For a pet with a superiority complex
QUEEN ANNE	For a pet that loves to sit on the furniture

QUEEN ELIZABETH	For a pet with family problems
QUEENIE	Michael Korda's book. Great dog name
QUEEN ISABELLA	For a pet that finances explorers
QUEEN LATIFAH	For a pet that likes to rap
QUENCHER	For a pet into Gatorade
QUENTIN	For a pet that understands *Pulp Fiction*
QUESADILLA	For a Mexican food lover
QUE SERA SERA	You're not sure it's purebred, but you're relaxed about it.
QUEST	For an American foxhound, bloodhound, coonhound, etcetera
QUETZAL	For a sweet, affectionate female
QUEUE	An English duck with its babies
QUIBBLER	A pet you can never satisfy
QUICHE	A real male won't eat it
QUICK	For a very smart pet
QUICKEN	A pet good at accounting
QUICKIE	For a stud animal
QUIET	For a pet you barely know is there
QUIGLY	Rhymes with wiggly ... must be a snake name
QUILL	For any bird
QUINCE	For a pet into exotic fruit
QUINCY	For an aspiring coroner
QUININE	A soothing pet
QUINN	For a mighty pet
QUIPSTER	A comedian's pet that never stops

QUIRK	For a pet with a tick
QUIXOTE	For a dreamer
QUIZ	For the pet that keeps you guessing
QUIZZIE	For a little pet that keeps you guessing
QUOGUE	A Hamptons aficionado
QUOTA	You swear it's your last pet.
QUOTH	Don't quoth me.

R2D2	For a pet that obeys your orders
RACER	A sailor's pet
RACEWAY	A greyhound
RADAR	For a "M*A*S*H" lover, or an air traffic controller
RADCLIFFE	Pair with Harvard
RADIO	For the pet that likes to switch channels
RAGGEDY ANDY	For a male ragdoll
RAGGEDY ANN	For a female ragdoll
RAGING BULL	A boxer
RAGS	For a sloppy pet
RAGTIME	For a pet that likes its "blanky"
RAGU	For a saucy pet
RAGWEED	For pets with runny eyes
RAIL	For a person who's as skinny as a . . .
RAILWAY	A conductor's pet
RAIN	An American water spaniel or any of the water dogs
RAINBOW	For a mixed breed

RAINER	Perhaps a great Spitz. Get it?
RAINWATER	A pet that won't drink from the toilet
RAINY	A dog that drools
RAISIN BREAD	A brown and white pet
RAJA	A posh Indian of great standing. A German shepherd or Doberman would be good.
RAKE	Definitely an unneutered, traveling man
RALEIGH	A smoker's pet
RALPH	Ralph Kramden . . . ''The Honeymooners.'' A wonderful pet name
RAMBO	Sylvester Stallone, look out! The name says it all!
RAMON	What a great name! How about for a pet that looks like it has a mustache?
RAMSEY	A strong name for a strong pet
RANDALL	A more selective ''Randy''
RANDY	A pet that's always ready for anything . . . another unneutered male
RANGER	For a pet that roams your land, or plays hockey
RANGE ROVER	A pet you can take anywhere
RAOUL	A cannibal's pet
RAPUNZEL	A puli would be perfection
RAQUEL	It would have to be a sexy animal, whatever it is.
RASHID	A pet that you're allergic to
RASKOLNIKOV	For the pet with a guilty conscience
RASPBERRY	A dog or cat with reddish hair would be adorable
RASTA	For a puli you have no intention of combing

RATATOUILLE   Perfect for a mutt

RATHBONE   For a pet that loves pesto

RAVEL   For a pet that wears a bolero

RAVIOLI   Stuffed pasta. A bichon frise!

RAY   One cool dude . . . sunglasses, possibly a hat, definitely connected

RAY CHARLES   For a singing animal that wants to do Pepsi commercials

RAYON   Someone in the ''rag trade'' could really do something with this name

RAZMATAZ   A flashy pet that looks good in a sequin collar

RAZOOK   For a pet that shrieks

RAZZ   For a pet that's fresh to its mother

RAZZMATAZZ   A dog that can do backward flips

REAGAN   For the pet that turns out differently than you expected

REAL ESTATE   Has no shame about advertising

REBECCA   The name of the poodle around the corner from me

REBEL   A pet for a hood from the sixties

RECALL   A pet for a person who would like to remember the sixties

RECCA   A nice way of naming an animal that wrecks your house

RECUPERATE   For someone partial to the ocean

RECYCLE   For a pet from the pound

RED   A red setter

RED CLOUD   A setter that lives on a reservation

RED CROSS   For a setter that thinks it's a Saint Bernard

RED EYE   For a bicoastal red setter

RED FIELD	For formal red setter
REDFORD	A setter that likes acting as your director
REDFURR	A well groomed red setter
REDNECK	For a red setter that only lives with its own kind
RED RIDING HOOD	A red setter that's always visiting its grandmother
RED SEA	For a setter that thinks it's Moses
REDWOOD	A setter that thinks it's exceptionally tall
REESE'S PIECE	A spotted tabby Egyptian mau
REFRIGERATOR	For the pet that loves its food
REFRY	A good name for a fish
REGGIE	A baseball player's pet
REGIS	*See* ''Doubles,'' Kathie Lee
REILLY	For someone who wants ''the life of . . .''
REISS	An Iceland dog
RELAY	A race dog
RELISH	A pet you got to go with your dachshund
REMBRANDT	For an artistic Dutch sheepdog
REMINGTON	A pet of ''Steele''
REMOTE CONTROL	For a pet that obeys when you call it
REMUS	Pair with Romulus
RENO	A divorced couple might consider this for their next pet
RENOIR	A painter's pet
REPETE	Pair with Pete
REPLAY	*See* ''Recall''

REPORTER	A newsperson's pet
REQUIEM	For a heavyweight
RESCUE	Saint Bernard, or any pet you get from the pound
RESCUER	Same, but it finds *you*
RESEARCH	For the pet that can never be found
RETAIL	A pet for a person who never buys wholesale
RETREAD	A name for an old dog from the pound
REUBEN	My elevator man . . . looks good in a uniform
REUTERS	A Russian wolfhound into the news
REVEREND	A black cat with a white collar
REWIND	A good name for anyone in the audio or video business
REX	Now here's an original name
RHAPSODY	For any of your blue breeds
RHETT	A dashing pet that doesn't give a damn
RHETT BUTLER	A dashing pet that doesn't give a damn and prefers a proper introduction
RHINESTONE COWBOY	A dalmatian. We'll pretend that all those spots are rhinestones.
RHUBARB	For a sourpuss
RHYMER	A poet's pet
RHYTHM	A musician's pet
RIBBON	For a snake
RIBBONS	A winner's pet
RICARDO	Pair with McGillicudy

RICHARD	Strange name for a pet. But, anything's possible.
RICK	Richard's nickname. For a *Casablanca* fan ... pair with Ilsa
RICKLES	For an acerbic pet
RICKRACK	A seamstress' pet
RICKSHAW	One of the Chinese dogs. A Shih Tzu or Lhasa apso, or a pet you can ride
RICKY	Lucy's sweetheart
RIDDLER	A pet that enjoys giving you trouble
RIDDLES	An obnoxious joke person's pet
RIGHTY	For a pet that's never wrongy
RILEY	For a William Bendix fan
RINGLING BROTHERS	If you can get all your pets to do the same trick simultaneously
RIN TIN TIN	This is actually a very weird name
RIO	For a grande pet
RIP	A name for a guard dog
RIPLEY	For someone with ten cats and gets another ... believe it or not
RIPTIDE	For a fast turtle
RIP VAN WINKLE	A name for a guard dog that sleeps on the job
RISKY	A Yugoslavian tricolor hound. Anything from Yugoslavia is a bit risky right now.
RISQUÉ	A hairless dog (cane nudo). That's the name, and it's found in Mexico.
RITZ	Possibility for a parrot. Ritz, as in cracker, as in "Polly"
RIVA	For someone with an accent
RIVER	Portuguese water dogs love swimming

RIXON	Son of Rick
RIZZO	Good for a hamster or rat
ROAD RUNNER	A jogger's name for his bird
ROAMER	*See* Rake
ROBERT REDFURR	Someone really named their cat this
ROBERTA	For a pet that gives no flack
ROBIN	For a bird or singing pet, or pair with Batman
ROBIN HOOD	A pet that takes your belongings and brings them to the neighbors
ROBINSON CRUSOE	A pet that can fend for itself
ROB ROY	A pet that fights for what it believes in
ROCCO	Another connected guy. Older than Ray
ROCHESTER	Jack Benny's sidekick
ROCK	For a strong, immovable animal
ROCKET J. SQUIRREL	Pair with Bullwinkle
ROCKETTE	For pets with particularly great legs
ROCKWELL	A pet for someone named Norman, or an engineer
ROCKY	Sylvester Stallone
ROCKY II	Sylvester Stallone
ROCKY III	Sylvester Stallone
ROCKY IV	Sylvester Stallone
ROCKY MOUNTAIN HIGH	Sylve . . . (oops) John Denver
ROCKY ROAD	A Russian wolfhound and an American shorthaired pointer mix

RODIN	An artist's pet
RODNEY	A cocker spaniel, or any pet that gets no respect
ROGER	Ann-Margret's favorite pet
ROGER RABBIT	For a rabbit with a career in the movies
ROGET	The pet you depend on when writing
ROGUE	This reminds me of the movie with David Niven. Chicly naughty
ROLAND	A great, big briard
ROLEX	When you can't buy one
ROLLER	A pet that likes the high life
ROLLERBLADE	A pet that likes the fast life
ROLLER SKATE	A pet that likes the old life
ROLLO	For a pet that may
ROLLO MAY	For the pet that will help you be your best self
ROLY-POLY	For a pet that starts out fat and will stay that way
ROMAINE	A pet that likes green vegetables
ROMAN	For an Italian pointer
ROMEO	Romeo, oh, Romeo. Pair with Juliet. Shakespeare would be happy, but the Capulets will be upset with you.
ROMI	For a pet that hates to stay home
ROMULUS	Pair with Remus
RONALD	Nancy won't like you
RONNIE	Nancy will really hate you now
RONNO	For a disobedient Ron
ROOFER	For a dog that goes ''roof roof'' (sorry)
ROOSEVELT	I like this name. It has character. Maybe a basset hound or a mastiff

ROPER	A cowboy's pet
RORSCHACH	A pet whose markings always remind you of something
ROSA	Your Spanish pet looks good with one between its teeth
ROSANNA	For a pet with a sweet, kind disposition
ROSANNA-DANNA	A pet that watches "Saturday Night Live" reruns
ROSCOE	This reminds me of someone at the track. So, I would say, a better's pet.
ROSE	Your American pet looks good with one between its teeth
ROSEANNE	An adorable bulldog with lots of money and power
ROSEDALE	A pet from the suburbs
ROSENKRANTZ	Pair with Guildenstern
ROSIE	In my opinion, one of the nicer female names
ROSIE O'GRADY	Another good name for a Great Dane or any other large animal
ROSIE THE RIVETER	A female bulldog
ROSKO	A wirehaired fox terrier or any frisky pet
ROTINI	More pasta
ROULETTE	For any caged animal that has a wheel
ROUSSEAU	A jungle animal
ROVER	A dog that won't stay in its own backyard
ROWDY	A Bosnian hound
ROWENA	A white Oriental shorthair

ROWF	For the dog that named itself
ROWSER	A pet for someone who finds it hard to wake up
ROXANNE	Pair with Cyrano
ROXETTE	An ex-Rockette
ROXIE	An old movie aficionado's pet
ROY	The husband of my cousin in Connecticut but still one of the great pet names, too
ROY BOY	What she calls him
ROYCE	Rolls' last name
ROY ROGERS	Dale Evans and Trigger's best friend
ROZA	A South American pet that looks good with a rose in between its teeth
RUBLE	For a worthless animal
RUBY	For pets born in July
RUBY FRUIT	For a July pet with exotic tastes, or any pet that appreciates jewels
RUDEBOY	For a fresh and sassy pet
RUDOLPH	If you have a reindeer, perfection
RUDY	Nickname for a pet with antlers
RUFF	Dennis the Menace's dog
RUFFER	A roofer's pet
RUFFHAUSER	A Rottweiler, German shepherd, vizsla, or any pet that plays too hard
RUFFIAN	A pet with a dirty-looking face
RUFUS	Such a perfect animal name
RUGBY	For pets that look good in shorts
RUGGELAH	For a pet who gains weight over the holidays
RUGGLES	A pet who waddles ... especially appropriate for short-legged varieties

RUM	Pair with Coke
RUMBA	Great name for a dachshund. Can't you just picture those tiny legs swinging around?
RUMMY	For a pet that loves gin
RUMOR	For a talking bird that loves gossip
RUMPEL-STILTSKIN	Another good name for the Shar-pei
RUNNER	A greyhound
RUNWAY	A pilot's pet
RUNYON	For any racing animal
RUPERT	For a media mogul
RUSH	A mynah bird with two right wings
RUSHMORE	For a pet with a granite face
RUSS	A short, athletic type
RUSSELL	The second most favorite name of the Jack Russell terrier. The first, as you can guess, is Steve. (Just kidding.)
RUSTY	Always makes me think of ''The Danny Thomas Show''
RUTHIE	For an indoor cat
RYAN	The pet for which you have hope
RYDER	For a pet that's always on the move
RYE	Pair with Hamon
RYLEE	An Irish terrier with a southern accent

SABATINI	For a tennis buff
SABIN	An inoculator's pet
SABRINA	One of "Charlie's Angels"
SABU	For a big, clumsy-looking pet ... like a Saint Bernard, Clumber spaniel, or Newfoundland
SADAT	For an Egyptian sphynx
SADIE	Married lady. For the nonspaded female, maybe?
SADIE HAWKINS	Feline seeking male companion
SADONA	A psychic's pet
SAFIRE	For an opinionated pet
SAGAN	An extraterrestrial pet
SAGE	For a very wise pet or a spicy one
SAGGY	Perfect for a basset hound or a Sharpei
SAHARA	For a camel
SAHL	Comic dog from the Lenny Bruce era
SAILOR	For a black and white animal ... mostly white

SAINT	For a perfect pet whose owner is named Eva or Marie
SAINT LAURENT	For a pet that walks like it's on a runway
SAL	For a pet into pizza
SALAZAR	For a long distance runner
SALES	A salesman's pet
SALINGER	For a French bulldog, or a hermit
SALISBURY	For a pet into steak
SALK	For a pet into shots
SALLY	And Buddy from ''The Dick Van Dyke Show''
SALOME	For a pet that needs seven veils or wants your head on a platter
SALVADOR	For a Dalí
SAM	A no-nonsense pet. Another of the all-time greats
SAMANTHA	A no-nonsense female, Sam's formal name
SAMMY	What you call the no-nonsense Sam when you're happy with him
SAMPRAS	Tennis again
SAMSON	For any of the very big- (or very small), very long- (or very short) haired breeds ... preferably shaggy.
SAM SPADE	A no-nonsense, neutered pet that does detective work on the side
SAM WAH	A no-nonsense Chinese crested dog
SAND	A pet that sticks in your craw
SANDBURG	A poet's pet
SANDER	A floor finisher's pet
SANDERS	A colonel's pet

SANDOR	For someone with very clear pronunciation
SANDY	The scruffy dog featured in *Annie*
SANIBEL	For an island pet
SAN PELLEGRINO	For a pet that only drinks bottled water
SANTA	For a jolly, fat pet
SANTA CLAWS	For a jolly, fat pet with claws
SANTA FE	An artist's pet partial to turquoise
SANTANA	A guitarist's pet
SAPPHIRE	From the TV show "Amos and Andy"
SAPPHO	A-museing pet
SARABETH	For a pet with braids
SARAH	For a blue-cream point Himalayan . . . no braids
SARATOGA	For a horse that races
SARGENT	For a guard dog
SARNO	For a pet with good skin
SARNOFF	A dalmatian that likes to watch TV
SAROYAN	For a borzoi, Russian blue, Russian wolfhound, etcetera
SARTO	For an artsy pet
SARTRE	For an existential pet
SASHA	For a Russian bird into teasing helpless wolves
SASHIMI	For a sushi fan (it also happens to be one of my ex-husband's cats)
SASSAFRAS	For a pet with a keen sense of smell
SASSOON	For a pet that likes to go to the groomer often
SASSY	For a pet that talks back

SATCHEL	For a pet that's going to be carried around a lot, one that plays baseball
SATCHMO	For a Newfoundland with a raspy voice
SATIE	For the pet that loves French composers
SATIRE	A mangy pet, but you insist on a sequined collar and pink bows for its hair
SAUCERS	For a pet with big eyes
SAUL	For a pet that bellows
SAUVIGNON	A wine lover's pet
SAVALAS	For someone into bald eagles and lollipops
SAVANNAH	For a pet from Georgia
SAWYER	For a tomcat
SAY SO	For a pet that likes the last word
SAY WHAT	For a hard-of-hearing cat
SCAASI	A designer's pet
SCANDAL	What you get when you cross a pedigree with a mixed breed
SCARECROW	And Mrs. King . . . perfect for a barn cat
SCARLATTI	For a pet with papers
SCARLETT	For a willful pet
SCARLETT O'HARA	For a willful pet with good taste in men
SCAVULLO	For a pet that likes to have its picture taken
SCHEHERAZADE	For a pet that really knows how to tell a story
SCHELL	A fancy fish
SCHIAPARELLI	A designer's pet

SCHIPA	For a Dutch border collie with its own flock
SCHIPPERS	For someone who works in a moving company
SCHLEMMER	Hammacher's partner
SCHLES	Slessinger's nickname
SCHLESINGER	For a very formal, politically minded person
SCHMIDT	For a Doberman or German shepherd
SCHMOODER	For one of the very hyper terriers
SCHNAPSIE	For a schnauzer that drinks
SCHNEIDER	Another good terrier name. No nonsense but yet . . .
SCHOONER	A sailor's pet
SCHOPEN-HAUER	For one of the giant breeds, preferably German, preferably musical
SCHRIMP	For one of the mini breeds, silky terrier, chihuahua, Cairn terrier
SCHUBERT	For an alley cat
SCHULTZ	Pair with Hogan or Klink
SCHULZ	For a *Peanuts* fan
SCHUMAN	A musician's pet
SCHUSTER	Pair with Simon
SCHWAR-ZENEGGER	Another one for a giant breed, preferably Austrian, preferably a guard dog
SCHWEITZER	African tsetse fly
SCONE	For someone who enjoys high tea in England
SCOOBY DOO	A cartoon character in the form of a dog
SCOOP	A journalist's pet
SCOOT	Scooter's nickname

SCOOTER	For someone who likes pie
SCORSESE	A director's pet
SCOTCH	A drinker's pet
SCOTT	Scottish terrier. What else?
SCOTTIE	A Scottish terrier would be the obvious choice; for a person with sinus problems, less obvious
SCOTTO	For a good ole boy Scottish terrier
SCOUNDREL	For that naughty pet
SCOUT	For an American bloodhound
SCRABBLE	For a pet that's smarter than you are, or one that needs its nails trimmed
SCRAMBLER	For a Cairn terrier . . . or any pet that slides on the hardwood floor
SCRUNCH	For a tawny boxer, Shar-pei, Pekingese, or pug
SEA BREEZE	Great drink, mellow atmosphere, good memories
SEAGAL	A martial arts lover's pet
SEAGRAM	A drinker's pet
SÉANCE	For a black cat
SEBASTIAN	My sister-in-law had two Old English sheepdogs . . . both were named Sebastian
SEDAKA	For someone that's just been through a divorce (breaking up is hard to do)
SEDRICK	One of the great names
SEEGER	A folk singer's pet
SEE TING	For a party planner
SEGA	A new age game pet
SEGOVIA	A guitarist's pet
SELES	A tennis player's pet

SELLECK	For a very good-looking pet that doesn't take itself too seriously
SELMA	A civil rights worker's pet
SELTZER	For a bubbly pet
SELWYN	The name's been in the family for years, and you can't get out of it now
SENATE	For a very stately, calm pet
SENATOR	For a not-so-calm pet that needs to be leashed
SENOR	For a Spanish mastiff
SERGEI	For an Italian pointer
SERLING	For a pet you're beginning to think came from "The Twilight Zone"
SETTLER	When you end up with the runt of the litter
SEUSS	A doctor's pet, or cat in a hat
SEVAREID	A TV newsperson's pet
SEVENTH HEAVEN	When you've avoided "Settler" and gotten your pick
SEVERINSEN	A trumpet playing Doc-shund
SEYMORE	For someone with good eyesight
SEYMOUR	A fat pet
SERGEANT PEPPER	For a lonely heart
SHADE	An evening pet. Wouldn't this be great for a black Lab?
SHADOW	Follows you wherever you go
SHAH	An exiled pet
SHAKESPEARE	A poetic pet
SHANDLING	A comic pet
SHANE	A horse ... any pet from the West
SHANGRI-LA	An easy-to-be-with pet

SHANKAR	A Ravi fan
SHANNEN	A 90210 fan
SHARIF	An Omar fan
SHATNER	A Trekkie fan
SHATZI	A wirehaired fox terrier
SHATZY	A small Swiss hound
SHAW	For a pharaoh hound ... docile, loyal, affectionate, and playful
SHAWN	For any of the Irish breeds
SHEENA	For the queen of the jungle
SHEFFIELD	The father on ''The Nanny,'' so for any pet that's sort of snobby
SHEIK	For a very suave pet, preferably with Arabic heritage
SHELBY	An aspiring preppy's pet
SHELDON	A pet that gives you reason to have *Memories of Midnight*
SHELLY	For a cute fish
SHEP	A name for a German shepherd given by an owner always in a hurry
SHEPHERD	For any of the sheepdogs that look good with a staff
SHERATON	A hotel lover's pet
SHERBERT	For a multicolored pet
SHERIDAN	An Ann fan
SHERIFF	Another good name for a guard dog
SHERMAN	For a pet built like a tank
SHERWOOD	For a ''Murphy Brown'' wanna be
SHEVARDNADZE	For any of the Russian breeds
SHIH LIANG	For a Lhasa apso, Shih Tzu, etcetera
SHINER	For a dog or cat with one black eye

SHIRLEY	Shirley basset hound
SHISH KEBAB	For any of the breeds with particularly short legs . . . dachshunds, corgis, etcetera
SHOCKING BLUE	You thought it was going to be a red point Birman.
SHOCKING PINK	You thought it was going to be a blue point Birman.
SHOGUN	For any of the Japanese breeds
SHOOKER	A pet you always have to wake up
SHOOTING PAIN	A pet that gets in the way of your target practice
SHORTIE	Any short pet, or, to be contrary, any very tall pet
SHOWBOAT	For the pet that likes old musicals
SHOW-OFF	For the pet that always takes first prize, then brags about it
SHRIVER	Pam, Sargent, and Eunice
SHUBI	For someone partial to fifties songs
SICILY	For an Italian hound, very proud of its heritage
SID	Nondenominational and adorable
SIDNEY	Nondenominational and still adorable
SIEGFRIED	Pair with Roy
SIEPI	For an Italian hound . . . vivacious but undemonstrative in affection
SIGGI	For a small spitz . . . affectionate with family, suspicious of strangers
SIGMUND	A therapist's pet
SIGNORET	A pet for a Simone
SILICONE	Either for a valley pet, or one with implants

SILKY Any of the terriers ... Australian, Silky, or any pet that merits the title

SILVER SPIRIT For a silver mackerel ... or any beautiful gray pet

SIMBA A pet from the jungle

SIMMONS For a bubbly, bouncy pet that's into dieting

SIMON A pet that makes you do as it says

SIMONE For a Signoret fan

SIMPSON For a pet that can keep a straight face under any circumstances, or a Bart lover

SINATRA Ole blue eyes. Great for a husky

SINBAD A sailor's pet

SINCLAIR Good name for a strong, dependable pet, Pyrenees mastiff, Newfoundland, American foxhound

SINGER Any of the bird breeds

SINSO For floppy pets with long, hanging ears

SIREN For a pet that howls

SIR STUD For a prolific pet with class

SISLEY For someone in the tie business

SITTING BULL For a sitting bull (sorry, I had to)

SKEET A shooter's pet

SKEETER Because your heart *must* go on beating, that's why

SKEET SHOOT For a duck

SKELETON For a Devon rex or a greyhound

SKELTON For a red pet

SKIPPER For a "Gilligan's Island" fan

SKIPPY For a peanut butter addict

SKY	A pilot's pet
SKY KING	For someone with over one million frequent flier miles
SLEEPING BEAUTY	For a pet that naps a lot and likes apples
SLIM	For a greyhound
SLIM PICKINS	What's left of the greyhound's litter
SLOAN'S	A supermarket I worked in the summer before college
SLY	For a sneaky pet
SMIRNOFF	Less expensive than Stoli
SMITH	For a pet that wants to be incognito
SMITHIE	For an incognito pet that wants a nickname
SMITS	For a police dog
SMITTIE	For a rookie police dog
SMOCKING	For a tabby
SMOKEY	Perfect for a Newfoundland, or someone named Robinson
SMYTH	For a fancy Smith
SMYTHE	For a fancy Smith who's English
SNAPPLE	For a pet that drinks a lot
SNEAKERS	For a pet that creeps up on you all the time
SNOOPY	Is he a beagle?
SNOWBALL	For an all-white kitten
SNOWDON	Lord, I don't know
SNOWFLAKE	For an all-white kitten that's one of a kind
SNOWMAN	For a Siberian husky
SNOWSHOE	An Eskimo dog

SNOW WHITE	The last and largest in a litter of eight tiny animals
SNYDER	For a giant schnauzer
SO BIG	For a Yorkie
SOCKS	Any pet with markings around its paws
SOCRATES	Any pet that thinks a lot
SODA	Companion to Scotch
SOHO	For a trendy pet from New York City
SOJOURNER	For a tomcat
SOLACE	The pet you buy to replace someone else
SOLDIER	A boxer or bulldog
SOLO	Any pet that likes to be alone
SOLO MAN	For a one-pet family
SOLOMON	For a serious pet
SOLZHENITSYN	Another name for any of the Russian breeds
SONA	A friend's cocker spaniel, whose nickname is Precious
SONAR	For a pet bat
SONDHEIM	For a pet that wants to be on Broadway
SONTAG	For a black pet with a white streak
SOON PENG	An akita, Tibetan mastiff, Shar-pei, etcetera
SOPHIE	You had a choice
SOPHOCLES	A pet into drama or Greek tragedies
SOUFFLÉ	For someone into desserts
SOUPY	For someone into soups
SOURDOUGH	For someone into bread

SOUSA	For a marching band leader's pet
SPACEY	For someone into drugs
SPARKIE	For someone into matches
SPARKLE	For someone into fireworks
SPARKS	For someone into fires
SPARKY	For someone into starting fireworks
SPAULDING	For someone into tennis
SPECTATOR	For a voyeur's pet
SPECTRUM	For someone into colors
SPECULATOR	For someone into the stock market
SPENDER	For a shopper's pet
SPENSER	A detective's pet
SPIDER MAN	For someone into climbing the walls, or a pet that eats insects
SPIEGEL	For someone into catalog shopping
SPIKE	For a Dandie Dinmont terrier (has just one tuft of hair on its head)
SPIKE LEE	For a Dandie Dinmont terrier that directs movies
SPILLANE	A detective's pet, or for a macho hunting dog that wears a hat indoors
SPINOZA	A philosopher's pet
SPIRIT	For a make-believe pet
SPIVAK	For any of the Russian breeds
SPLASH	For a mermaid . . . or, how you know the cat's in the fish tank again
SPOCK	A Vulcan breed with big, pointy ears
SPODE	A delicate, almost breakable pet
SPOILER	For a bratty bulldog
SPOOK	Mrs. Muir's captain
SPOOKY	That Mrs. Muir *had* a captain

SPORT	A jock's pet
SPOT	Belongs to Dick and Jane
SPRING	For any pet that arrived in the early part of the year
SPRINGSTEEN	The Boss' pet
SPRITE	Any pet that likes clear sodas
SPUTNIK	An astronaut's pet
SPY	A mysterious pet
SPYMASTER	For an espionage fan
SQUASH	A flat pet
SQUAW	An Indian pet
SQUEAK	A tiny pet
SQUEAKIE	A teeny pet
SQUIRT	A small pet
STACKER	A strong pet
STADIUM	For the sports fan who thinks of a pet as a mascot
STAKEOUT	For a very patient watchdog
STALACTITE	A pet with floppy ears
STALAGMITE	A pet with pointy ears
STALLONE	A rocky pet
STANLEY	An ice hockey fan's pet
STANWYCK	For a dramatic pet
STAR	A famous pet, or a horse with a blaze on its forehead
STARBUCK	A pet into coffee
STARDUST	A dead famous pet
STAR FIRE	A rising famous pet
STAR FROST	An outdoor famous pet
STARR	An extra famous pet

STEELE	For someone who loved "Remington Steele"
STEINBECK	For a red pony or a pet partial to grapes
STELLA	A *Streetcar* fan
STERLING	For a pet that eats from a silver bowl
STETHOSCOPE	A pet snake with sensitive hearing
STETSON	The pet that looks good in cowboy hats
STEVENS	For a "Bewitched" fan
STEVENSON	A Democrat's pet ... pair with Eisenhower
STEWARD	For someone who likes to take cruises
STEWART	For someone who likes Martha
STING	For someone who likes bees
ST. JAMES	A religious pet
STOCKARD	A guard dog
STOCKWELL	A dean's pet
STOKES	For a pet into fires
STOLI	*See* Smirnoff
STONE	This is for one tough pet
STONY	For a very stubborn pet
STORMIN' NORMAN	A survey showed that an overwhelming majority of women said they would most like to be stranded on an island with him. Can you believe it?
STOSSEL	For someone who seeks the truth
STRADIVARI	A pair of pets in tune with you
STRADIVARIUS	A pet that is in tune with you
STRAUSS	For a pet that waltzes
STRAVINSKY	A musician's pet

STRAWBERRY	An athlete's pet, a cook's pet, or a pet for someone in rehab
STREEP	A cat that's such a good actress that you sometimes think it's a dog
STREISAND	A ballad-belting Afghan that pays close attention to details
STRETCH	A limo-riding dachshund
STRITCH	For a baby limo-riding dachshund
ST. TROPEZ	For a topless pet
STUART	A Scottish clan dog ... pretensions to the throne. For any pet trying to creep up the evolutionary ladder
STUDS	For a flashy pet ... sort of a rhinestone cowboy
STURGES	Another good Scottish name for someone into ''they don't make 'em like that anymore'' movies
STUTZ	A Bearcat
STUYVESANT	For a Peter
SUDS	A clean pet
SUE	For a boy named
SUEDE	Any of the blue breeds
SUEY PING	An eastern pet
SUGAR	A southern pet
SUGARLOAF	A skier's pet
SUGAR RAY	A boxer
SUKI	An Asian pet
SULLIVAN	An Irish pet
SULLY	An Italian pet
SULTAN	An Arab pet
SULTANA	A yellow, wrinkled pet
SUMO	A Japanese fighting pet

SUMMER	A hot pet
SUMMER BREEZE	A hot pet with a cool temperament
SUMMER STOCK	For a pet that likes revivals
SUNBONNET	A pet with a flat top and bushy eyebrows
SUN DANCE	A pet from a rainy climate
SUNFLOWER	A pet with a big face and a crown of hair
SUNG	A pet with big lungs
SUNNY	For a happy pet
SUN RA	A jazz musician's pet
SUNRISE	A pet shaded from red to orange to yellow
SUNRISE, SUNSET	For a pair from the shelter
SUNSET	A pet shaded from yellow to orange to red
SUNSHINE	A pet without PMS
SUN YAT-SEN	For a pet into Chinese history
SUPERMAN	A pet that doesn't mind hanging out with a nonsunshine animal
SURE BET	For a greyhound
SURPRISE	For an unexpected addition
SUSANNAH	For someone into banjos
SUSHI	For someone into fish
SUSSKIND	For someone into David
SUTHERLAND	For someone into Donald
SUZETTE	For someone into crepes
SUZUKI	For someone into motorcycles or violin lessons

SVENGALI	An older pet you're still breeding
SVETLANA	For someone into Russians
SWAYZE	For someone into dancing
SWEET GEOR-GIA BROWN	For someone into golden oldies
SWEET GINGER	For someone into the *Flamingo Kid*
SWEETHEART	For a sentimentalist
SWEETIE PIE	For a pet with just a little of the rascal in it
SWEET PEA	Popeye's baby
SWEET POTATO	For a red pet: red Abyssinian, Oriental red, Irish setter
SWEET WILLIAM	For any sweet-looking, mellow pet
SWIFT	A pet for a Jonathan
SWIFTIE	Another good greyhound name
SWIFTY	A pet just this side of the law
SWISS BLISS	A chocolate lover's pet
SWISS MISS	A cocoa lover's pet
SWIT	Another name for a "M*A*S*H" fan
SWOOZIE	For a pet who faints easily
SYBIL	A pet with multiple personalities
SYLVESTER	A cat, of course
SYLVIA	Another of my favorite pet names ... any female pet would be suitable

3-D	For a pet whose eyes are two different colors
T.C.	The Cat
T.J.	Tough, athletic type
T.K.O.	A boxer
T.R.	The Runt
TAB	A hunter's pet
TABBY	Striped cats
TABITHA	Striped cats with stuck-up tails and a lisp
TABLESPOON	Big animals that share your food at mealtimes
TACO	For anyone who loves Mexican food
TAFFETA	An animal that rustles as it goes by
TAFFY	What girls aged five to eight name their cocker spaniels
TAFT	United States president (1909–1913). Chief justice (1921–1930)
TAGS	A pet that won't leave your side. Either that or it bears a strong resemblance to your luggage

T'AI CHI   Chow chows, Pekingese, Siamese, etcetera

TAIGA   For a tiger with a New York accent

TAILOR   Best used in collections . . . companions are Tinker, Soldier, and Spy

TAI PAN   A Chinese imperial Ch'in . . . the leader

TAJ   For a Mahal

TAKAHO   For a Japanese spitz

TAKEOUT   A city pet

TALBOT   Old English sheepdogs, Irish wolfhounds

TALLCHIEF   The female Native American ballet dancer . . . though American, an Afghan would be perfect

TALLEYRAND   The French statesman (1754–1838). A beagle, perhaps?

TALLULAH   For your most dramatic pet

TALMUD   For a Yiddish owl

TAMALE   For a hot Chihuahua

TAMARA   One of my grandmothers, but I also see it for a female Siamese.

TAMBOURINE   Those with collars holding many I.D. tags

TAMIL   Indian and Sri Lankan race and language

TAMMY   Cute and bouncy . . . like a bichon frise

TAM O' SHANTER   For Scotties

TANDY   For a pet that mates for life

TANGLEWOOD   For pulis

TANGO   You two should be very close

TANK	Guard dogs. A tough guy's companion
TANKARD	Your drinking companion
TANKER	A nice, fat pet
TANKER RAY	A nice, fat pet named Ray that drinks gin
TAN POY	For a Chinese crested dog
TANTE	For a German shepherd or a German pointer . . . means "aunt" in German
TANTRA	A cat name
TANTRUM	For the pet that acts out
TANYA	A competitive pet, though not recommended as an ASA show animal
TAO	A pet with many secrets, or one that is at one with itself
TAOS	For reptiles
TAPESTRY	For animals with coats that tell a story
TAPIOCA	Off white with little fur balls
TAPPER	Any cat with socks
TAPSHOE	A pet whose nails are left unclipped
TARA	Home for Scarlett
TARGET	Dalmatians and leopards
TARIFF	Expensive and imported
TARKINGTON	American writer . . . perfect for a Newfoundland, big dog, big name
TAROT	A symbolic pet
TARRAGON	An animal partial to meat and poultry
TARZAN	For a pet that keeps going out looking for Jane
TASHI	A Lhasa apso
TASTER	Any pet that shares your food

TATE For a lovable but slightly dingy pet (I loved "Soap" and Jessica Tate)

TATER TOT One of Tate's kids

TATI A tall French poodle that is funny (French director and actor Jacques Tati)

TATIANA For a pet that smells good

TATTOO A pet with distinctive markings, at least one of which looks like a heart with the word MOM in it

TAURUS For a very stubborn pet, or one born in May

TAXI Horses, mules, elephants, or camels

TAX SHELTER A very expensive animal you can write off

TAYLOR For an Elizabeth, Robert, Renee, Zachary, or Miss Taylor (your third grade teacher)

TAZZA For a miniature breed ... something that can fit in a cup

TCHAIKOVSKY For borzois, Russian blues, and swans

TEA BISCUIT For lap dogs

TEACHER'S PET When you've chosen the runt of the litter

TEAPOT An animal with a stiff tail

TEASDALE American poet. A pet that plays hide-and-seek

TEASPOON Little animals that share your food at mealtimes

TECUMSEH Parrots, macaws, etcetera

TED For a no-nonsense animal

TEDDY Softer and cuter than Ted

TEDDY BEAR	Softer and cuter than Teddy (with a paunch)
TEENY WEENY	One of those double names whose second half you'll never get around to using
TEKA MAKI	For a fish that won't be cooked
TELEGRAM	For a homing pigeon
TELEPATHY	For a pet that anticipates your every command
TELEX	The homing pigeon's younger brother
TELLER	Caged animals
TELLY	Shaved head, likes lollipops
TEMPEST	Any pet that fits in a teapot
TEMPLETON	The rat from the children's classic *Charlotte's Web*
TEMPO	Upbeat or downbeat, whatever your fancy
TENNESSEE	Horses and owners that know how to spell
TENNILLE	Alone, it rhymes with a schlemiel . . . paired with the Captain, it still rhymes
TENNIS ANYONE	A tennis fanatic's pet
TENNYSON	A literary pet
TENOR	Heavyset male dogs with large egos
TEOK FU	Chinese Shar-pei
TERENCE	A stamp collector's pet
TERESA	Animal with a halo
TERIYAKI	For a saucy pet
TERKEL	For a stud
TERMINATOR	German shepherds, Doberman pinschers, and pit bulls

TERRA-COTTA	An animal to match your kitchen floor
TERRY	Shaggy coats . . . Samoyeds, Angoras
TESIA	For a golden Persian
TESLA	An underappreciated inventor (1856–1943)
TESSIE	Looks like your great aunt
TEST PILOT	Must look good with helmet and goggles
TETHYS	Goddess of the sea . . . best fish in the tank
TEX	Largest example of its species
TEXAS RANGER	A guard dog
TEXTBOOK	A perfect example of its breed
THACKERAY	English writer . . . wonderful pet name
THADDAEUS	Apostle also known as Saint Jude . . . also a wonderful pet name
THAI	A pet from Thailand
THALASSA	Pretentious name for a fish
THALBERG	Movie executive (1899–1936)
THALIA	Muse of comedy and poetry . . . one of the three graces
THANK YOU	Will establish a slightly formal but loyal relationship
THARP	Either you're partial to the dancer or you have a lisp
THATCHER	For an English bulldog
THAXTER	Great name for a male pet
THE GRADUATE	Mrs. Robinson's pet
THELMA	Neater than Louise
THEO	Van Gogh's brother. Ears intact
THEODORABLE	It's too adorable

THEODORAKI	It's too ridiculous
THEODORE	Fabulous name
THEORY	Explains your crossbreed
THERAPY	A good listener
THERMAL	Persians, Angoras, any warm, hairy animal
THERMOS	Reminds you of your lunchbox. For a pet that can stand extremes in the weather
THESEUS	Slayed the Minotaur
THESPIAN	One of you has a dramatic flair
THICK	A pet that has a dense coat
THIMBLE	For itty-bitty animals
THIN	*See* "Doubles," Thick and Thin
THISBE	Ill-fated lover of Pyramus. Bad ending
THOMAS	Likes English muffins
THOMAS MAGNUM	Likes Champagne with its English muffin
THOMPSON	A type of gun, a type of grape, your second grade teacher
THOR	Norse god of thunder . . . wonderful for the larger breeds
THOREAU	Animals that take care of themselves
THORN	A pet you regret
THORNDIKE	Scholarly
THORNEY	The queen bee
THORNY	The worker bee
THRILLER	Eyes and teeth that glow in the dark
THROCK-MORTON	The Great Gildersleeve

THUG	Tough and hairless ... a bulldog, pug, or Chinese Shar-pei. A Chihuahua would be funny.
THUMBELINA	Fairy tales and Danny Kaye
THUMBTACK	Sharp teeth, sharp claws
THUMPER	A character from *Bambi*. For any rabbit, of course
THUNDER	My friend's Great Dane. His brother was Lightning.
THUNDERBIRD	Beautiful example of its species
THURBER	Any pet would be flattered
THURGOOD	An animal with courage
THURMAN	For a basset hound
THURMOND	Your pet hawk
THURSDAY	When all else fails, resort to the day you got it
THYME	Likes double entendre
TIARA	Cockatoos, cockatiels
TIBBETT	Hamster, gerbil, etcetera
TIBBI	The hamster, gerbil, etcetera's pet
TIBERIUS	Attack dogs, piranhas, moray eels
TICKET	Your entree
TIDBIT	An animal you'll never take seriously
TIDDLYWINKS	A whimsical name for a whimsical pet
TIEGS	Cover girl material
TIERNEY	My mother's favorite actress
TIFFANY	Thin and elegant
TIFFIN	Not so thin
TIFFY	Just plain fat

TIGER	Maybe it's the stripes, maybe the personality
TIGER LILY	As long as it's yellow
TIGGER	Cute and resembles a drawing of a little tiger
TILLIE	A Tennessee treeing brindle
TIM	A pal
TIMBUCTU	Where Tim is from, or replaces the first Timbuc
TIME OUT	It's not just a name, it's a concept.
TIMER	For the pet that wakes you up at the same time every morning
TIMEX	Gives a licking and keeps on ticking
TIMOTHY	For that formal relationship
TINA	Tough, sexy, slightly hoarse voice
TINKER	Likes to fix things
TINKER BELL	Peter Pan's fixer-upper
TINNIE	For a pet with a tin ear
TINY	Actually my huge friend Rolf's nickname. He's a banker, and they call him Tiny, so I see this for a Newfoundland.
TINY TIM	For a pet that tramples through the tulips
TIOMKIN	For a Russian blue
TIPPERARY	For Irish setters that have come a long way
TIPPI	For those pets that have a distinctive patch of color at the ends of paws, tails, etcetera . . . and like Hitchcock
TIPPY	For those pets with the markings that have never heard of Hitchcock
TISH	Captain of the cheerleaders

TISHA	Her real name
TITAN	Great Danes, Saint Bernards, bullmastiffs, or, for the pet owner with a sense of irony, for a Chihuahua
TITANIA	*A Midsummer Night's Dream*
TITO	Independent communist leader of Yugoslavia
TOAST	For a pet that receives kudos often
TOASTER	The pet that gives kudos often
TOBAGO	An island pet
TOBIAS	A Pyrenees mastiff
TOBY	Perfect for those whose gender is difficult to determine
TODD	More unusual than Ted and once married to Elizabeth Taylor
TODDY	Saint Bernards
TOFFEE	Any classic brown dog or cat
TOKAY	Dessert wine
TOKYO	A rose's pet
TOKYO ROSE	Doesn't speak well of your relationship
TOLEDO	Holy
TOLKIEN	For hobbits
TOLSTOY	For pets that are very long
TOM	*See* "Triples," Dick, Harry, and Tom
TOMAHAWK	Cockatoos, cockatiels, toucans, poodles with fancy cuts
TOM JONES	For a rather sloppy eater
TOMLIN	Parrots or mynah birds
TOMMY	WHO?
TOM THUMB	Double-paw animals

TONI	A female mobster's pet
TONTO	A loyal companion of few words
TONY	A male mobster's pet
TOODLES	A pet that's always taking off
TOODY	Muldoon's partner
TOOT	This is so cute. It would do for any pet.
TOOTSIE	You were told it was female, but you were told wrong.
TOPAZ	Yellow eyes
TOP HAT	For pets with black and white tails
TOPPER	My favorite TV show while growing up . . . Cosmo and the Kerbys
TOPSIE	Pulis with blond, curly hair
TOPSY	A pet with black curly hair, poodles or the Chinese crested dog . . . hairless except for a tuft of hair on top of its head
TORTELLINI	A tortoise
TORTONI	Bisque coloring
TORY	Because, try as you might, conservative doesn't work as a name
TOSCANINI	Italian conductor (1867–1957). For the classical music lover
TOSHI	For a Shih Tzu . . . say them together five times fast
TOSHIYUKI	Japanese spaniel
TOTAL RECALL	For a parrot or a pet elephant
TOTER	Any animal that can carry you
TOTO	For a pet that's left Kansas
TOUCHÉ	For a pet that's always one up on you

TOULOUSE	Animals whose body length is double the leg length .. dachshunds
TOUPEE	For the Mexican hairless ... hairless except for one tuft of hair on its head
TOY	The name of Zelda and F. Scott Fitzgerald's bloodhound
TOYNBEE	Toy anythings, poodles, etcetera
TRACER	For a bloodhound
TRACKER	Setters, retrievers, spaniels
TRACY	Goes well with Hepburn
TRAINER	Jogging companions, or animals that have wheels in their cages
TRAMP	Either you like Disney, or it stays out all night
TRANQUILIZER	For any pet that lowers your blood pressure
TRAPPER	For a ''M*A*S*H'' fan
TRAUB	For a water spaniel
TRAVELER	Because you can't leave home without it
TRAVIS	A McGee's pet, or a country western fan's pet
TRAVOLTA	An animal who's made a comeback
TREACHER	A fish
TREETOP	For those who don't live on the floor
TREKKER	*See* ''Doubles,'' Star and Trekker
TRENT	A singer's pet
TREVOR	For an Old English sheepdog, English mastiff
TRIBUTE	An animal that was given as a gift
TRICK OR TREAT	Raccoons, or the female you thought had been spayed
TRICKY DICK	Companion to Checkers

TRIGÈRE	A designer's pet
TRIGGER	Pet horse
TRIGGER HAPPY	How Roy Rogers felt every time he saw his horse
TRINI	Cute and rhythmic
TRINIDAD	For someone who likes vacationing there
TRIPP	A third generation nickname
TRIPPER	For a clumsy pet
TRISTAN	My friend Joy's horse. For the literary minded, pair with Isolde
TRISTAR	White wings with a name
TRIVIAL PURSUIT	A gerbil on its wheel
TROMBONE	Dachshunds
TROOPER	Your long walk companion
TROTSKY	Stay out of Mexico, or for a Russian horse
TROUBLE	Guard dogs, or any pet that refuses to be housebroken
TROY	Horses and Great Danes ... well, you can't hide in them, maybe behind them?
TROYANOS	Canaries
TRUCKER	Bulldogs
TRUCK STOP	A bulldog's home
TRUDEAU	A Canadian Mountie's mount
TRUE BLUE	A dog that has saved your life
TRUFFAUT	For the French poodle kept in puffy haircuts
TRUFFLES	A very chichi pet
TRUJILLO	For a pet that takes over the house

TRUMAINE	For a pet that's truly from New England
TRUMAN	A pet you never expected to keep. Or if it's your last pet, you can say, "The buck stops here."
TRUMBULL	For an English mastiff . . . big and majestic
TRUMP	For a bridge player, or for someone into The Donald
TRUMPET	Parrots or swans
TSAR	Russian wolfhound
TSARINA	Borzoi
TSETSE	Small, pesky animals
TUBBS	Pair with Sonny Crockett
TUCCI	For an Italian pointer
TUCKER	For a pet that can tire you out
TUCKET	Nan's pet
TUCSON	Reptiles
TUESDAY	A sexy pet
TUFF STUFF	An ironic choice. The animal isn't what it thinks it is.
TUFFY	For a bichon frise
TUGBOAT	The fat fish in the aquarium
TUGS	For a big dog that hasn't been leash trained
TUILERIES	For a French bulldog
TULIP	For a pet that walks on its tiptoes
TUNER	Canaries
TUNNEY	A boxer
TUPPIE	A Tupperware salesman's pet
TURBO	Strong, powerful dogs

TURK	A tough animal ... bulldog, pit bull, Maine coon
TURNER	Mastiff
TURNIP	For a Cairn terrier, or any pet that's two colored and kind of round
TURTLENECK	Chinese Shar-peis, pugs
TUSHA	Was my Lhasa apso, who turned nasty
TUSHINGHAM	Green eyed, big rump
TUSSAUD	For a waxy pet
TUTSI	For a pet from Central Africa
TUTTI-FRUTTI	Mixed breeds
TUTU	Light on its feet. Birds and cats
TV	This pet is good company, but you'll always feel a little guilty about it.
TWAIN	Great pseudonym
TWAINEY	What Twain's wife would call him
TWEED	English setters, certain calicos
TWEETY	Betrays a lack of imagination
TWEETY BIRD	Sylvester the cat's nemesis
TWIGGS	For a very thin pet
TWIGGY	Greyhounds, salukis
TWILIGHT	Russian blues, silver or blue Persians
TWINKIE	The dessert of choice in the fifties and sixties
TWINKLE	How I wonder where you are
TWITTY	Conway's pet
TWYLA	A dancer's pet
TYLER	Tippecanoe and ... any water spaniel
TYSON	For a pet that can impose its size
TZARKESH	A Russian blue

UBU	That dog at the end of certain TV programs
UDALL	For a basset hound . . . low to the ground and slow
UFFIZI	A gallery lover's pet
UFO	For a pet that's spacey
UGANDA	For a Rhodesian ridgeback
UGGAMS	For a small continental spaniel who likes to entertain
ULLMANN	For a pet that will ultimately Liv
ULRICK	For a German shorthaired pointer
ULTIMA	For a pet that wears makeup
ULTIMATE	The best pet
ULTRA	The even better pet
ULTRASONIC	For a very fast pet
ULYSSES	For a pet with a middle initial, perferably S
UMAR	For an Iceland dog
UMBER	For a shaded gold exotic shorthair
UMBERTO	For an Italian hound
UMBRELLA	For a pet you get on a rainy day

UMP	For a baseball fan
UMPIRE	For the family mediator
UNCLE	For a pet that can pin you down
UNCLE BEN	A rice lover's pet
UNCLE REMUS	For a pet that likes to tell stories
UNCLE SAM	A patriot's pet
UNCONSCIOUS	Any lethargic pet
UNDERCOVER	A spy's pet
UNDERDOG	The cartoon lover's pet
UNDERFOOT	For the pet you keep tripping over
UNDERGROUND	For a pet that shows resistance
UNDERWOOD	A typist's pet
UNGARO	For a designing pet
UNGER	For a very, very neat pet
UNION	For a pet of mixed parentage
UNION JACK	Another choice name for the Jack Russell terrier
UNITY	A peacekeeper
UNSER	Any pet that likes to race
UPBEAT	For a happy pet
UPDATE	For an aspiring newscaster
UPDIKE	For an aspiring writer
UPHILL	A new skier's pet
UPI	A journalist's pet
UPKEEP	For a pet that needs to go to the groomer more than once a month
UPROAR	A pet that causes pandemonium
UPSHOT	For a basketball fan
UPSTART	For a rascal
UPTIGHT	For a nervous, anxious pet

URANUS	A stargazer's pet
URBAN	A city pet living in the country
UREY	For a color pointed European shorthair or chartreux . . . a cat with nine lives
URIAH	For a heap of a pet
URIS	A very prolific pet with a penchant for description
URSA	For a Swedish elkhound, or a bearlike pet
URSULA	I always think of Andress.
USHER	The male dog that greets you at the door
USHERETTE	The female dog that greets you at the door
USTINOV	I always think of Peter.
USURPER	The pet that takes over the house
UTAH	For someone who wants to go west
UTOPIA	The ideal pet
UTRILLO	A painter's pet
UZI	For a riveting pet

VACCARO   For a slightly plump but ever exciting pet

VACUUM   For the pet that devours anything that falls to the ground

VADIM   For a Roger

VAGABOND   For a pet that wanders from place to place

VAIL   A West Coast skier's pet

VALACHI   For a pet with papers

VALDEZ   A pet from Alaska, or a pet that's oily

VALENTINE   For someone who liked *Scruples*

VALENTINO   For someone who likes either dressing well or old movies

VALENZUELA For someone into baseball

VALERY   For a French poodle

VALIANT   Another Chevy that bit the dust, or for an extremely brave pet

VALLEE   Not *How Green Was My* but for a Rudy

VALLI   The Russian form of Vallee

VAMP	For a female French poodle, or any pet that gets around
VAN	For a standard schnauzer
VANCE	For someone into politics
VAN CLIBURN	For someone into music
VANCOUVER	For someone into dams
VANDERBILT	For someone into Gloria
VAN DYCK	Arist's pet with a pointy beard
VANESSA	For a beautiful Persian
VAN GOGH	Artist's pet, or one that's missing an ear
VAN HEUSEN	For someone into shirts
VANILLA	For someone into music or ice cream. Any white pet
VANITY	Again, music
VANNA	For someone into letters
VANNA BROWN	For a long-haired brown tabby
VANNA WHITE	For a long-haired white tabby
VARGAS	For a pinup pet
VASCO	For a Da Gama fan
VASILY	Artist's pet
VASSA	For a German longhaired pointer that can't say "water" correctly
VAUDEVILLE	A pet for someone who remembers before 1930
VAUGHN	Ilia Kuriakian's partner
VEGA	For someone into Chevys
VEGAS	For someone into gambling
VELÁZQUEZ	For someone into history
VELVET	For someone blue

VENICE	For a water dog
VENUS	For someone into unattainable beauty
VENUS DE MILO	The formal name
VERA	What a good, solid female pet name
VERDI	For someone into music
VERDON	What you say when the whole family has finished dinner
VERMONT	An East Coast skier's pet
VERMOUTH	For someone into liquor
VERNE	For an American foxhound
VERNON	For a Tennessee treeing brindle ... the name just sounds like it's from Tennessee
VERRAZANO	For someone into bridges
VERSAILLES	For someone into palaces
VERTIGO	For someone into heights
VESPER	For someone into prayer
VESPUCCI	For someone into history
VESTA	For a Gordon setter
VETERAN	For a pet that looks like it's been through the war
VICAR	For someone into Miss Marple stories
VICEROY	For someone from the sixties into smoking, or any regal-looking pet
VICHY	For someone into water
VICKI	Pair with Tiny Tim
VICKIE	Same pronunciation, different spelling
VICTOR	For someone into transvestites
VICTORIA	*See* Victor
VICTORY	For someone into winning

VICTROLA   For someone into nostalgia

VIDA   For someone into life

VIDAL   For someone into hair

VIDEO   For someone into TV

VIDEO TAPE   A TV producer's pet, or someone into taping off TV

VIDOR   For a Yugoslavian tricolor hound

VIKING   For someone into gorgeous men

VILA   For someone into home repair

VILLA   For someone into the good life

VILLEROY   For someone into china

VINAIGRETTE   For a female French bulldog

VINCENT   What you call Vinny when you're mad at him

VINNY   Just one of the guys

VINTAGE   For a pet you plan to keep a long time

VINTON   Roses are red, my love

VIOLA   For an English cocker spaniel

VIOLET   Goes with all the other flower names ... triple with Daisy and Lily

VIRGIL   Definitely for one of the American breeds ... a serious and reliable pet

VIRGO   For someone into signs

VIRTUAL REALITY   A pet that you only need to deal with when wearing your helmet

VISA   For a pet that gets you into debt

VISCOUNT   For a Westphalian basset or someone into titles

VISCOUNTESS   For a Westphalian bassetess

VISHNEVSKAY   What a name. A borzoi or Russian wolfhound would be wonderful.

VISITOR	For someone who isn't sure he wants to keep the new pet
VISTA	For an outdoor pet
VIVALDI	For someone into the four seasons
VIVIAN	For a red Abyssinian
VIXEN	For a pet you can't resist
VJ	For a video jockey
VLADIMERE	A Russian blue shorthair
VLADIMIR	Same pronunciation, different spelling
VODKA	A longhaired Russian or a drinker's pet
VODKI	Vodka's pet name
VOGUE	For someone into sewing
VOIGHT	For a midnight cowboy
VOIT	For a plain ole cowboy
VOLARE	Nel blu di pinto del blu
VOLCKER	For an avid Fed watcher . . . pair with Greenspan
VOLGA	A river pet
VOLTA	For a Black Forest hound
VOLTAIRE	For anyone into drama
VONCE	A rascal in Yiddish
VONNEGUT	For a pet that leans toward satire and black humor
VON ZELL	Harry! "The Burns and Allen Show"
VOODOO	For a pet that acts possessed
VOYAGER	A pet that never stays home
VREELAND	A small spitz
VUITTON	For a French mastiff . . . with an initialed collar
VULCAN	For a Trekkie

W. C. FIELDS	For a pet with a big nose, rosy cheeks, and a slightly vulgar manner
WADDLER	For a duck
WADDY	For a cowboy fan
WADER	For a Portuguese water dog
WADSWORTH	For a long fellow ... wirehaired dachshund
WAFFLE	For someone who can't make a decision
WAFTER	For a pet with a strong gas problem
WAGER	A gambler's pet
WAGGER	For a very happy puppy
WAGNALL	For a funky pet
WAGNER	A composer's pet
WAGS	For a beagle. Such a cute name
WAGTAIL	A bird's name
WAHOO	A fish
WAH-WAH	A guitarist's pet
WAITER	For a penguin
WAIT LIST	For a hard-to-get pet
WALDEN	For a pet that lives by a pond

WALDO	For a pet you keep having to look for
WALDORF	For a salad lover
WALKER	A pet for a man named Johnny
WALKING PAPERS	For the pet you get after the divorce
WALLER	For a fat pet
WALLFLOWER	For the runt of the litter
WALLIS	A pet aspiring to the throne, or one that has queenly aspirations
WALL STREET	An investor's pet
WALLY	For the "Leave It to Beaver" fan
WALNUT	Small brown pet
WALPOLE	For a Lapphund . . . a Swedish dog, affectionate with children and distrustful of strangers
WALT	Good all-around name
WALTER	Another favorite name for a pet
WALTER BROWN	Another for the brown California spangled
WALTER MITTY	For a pet that daydreams
WALTON	For a "Waltons" fan
WALTZ	For someone who takes dancing lessons
WAMBAUGH	A storyteller's pet
WANAMAKER	A clothes horse
WANDA	A fish!
WANDERER	For a pet that won't stay put
WARD	Another nickname for Howard
WARDEN	Another one for a guard dog
WARFIELD	For a Yugoslavian tricolor hound
WAR HAWK	For any of your guard dogs

WARHOL	For a pet that likes canned food
WARING	For a mutt . . . as in blended
WARLOCK	Could it be for a black cat?
WARMONGER	For a Doberman
WARMUP	A jogger's pet
WARNER	For a dog that barks every time someone is at your door
WARPATH	My parents, when I told them I bought a dog
WARREN	For an American foxhound
WARRIOR	For a tawny Great Dane or any of the larger breeds
WART	Does your pet have bad skin?
WARWICK	For someone into the psychic world
WASHINGTON	For someone with political aspirations
WASSAIL	For people who drink to your health
WATCHDOG	The yappier small dogs
WATCHER	From the book of the same name, it would have to be a golden retriever
WATERBERRY	For an American water spaniel
WATER BOY	For someone really into football
WATERGATE	For someone partial to the Nixon years . . . or not
WATERPROOF	For a duck or fish
WATERS	For any of the retrievers
WATSON	Pair with Holmes
WATTS	For a California type
WATUTSI	For someone who was a teenager in the sixties
WAVE DANCE	For a brown California spangled

WAVY	For a dog with curls ... puli, poodle, etcetera
WAXY	For a pet that looks like it just got waxed ... any of the hairless breeds
WAYNE	For a cowboy, or a Newton fan
WEATHERMAN	For the pet that refuses to go out when it's raining
WEAVER	Dennis or Sigourney fans
WEBER	For a duck, or a pet that likes to grill
WEBSTER	A good speller's pet
WEDGEWOOD	For a very delicate pet
WEDNESDAY	For a pet you buy on a Wednesday
WEEKENDER	For the pet that goes with the kids every other weekend
WEEPER	For any pet that drools excessively
WEEZER	Good for a pug, for obvious reasons
WEEZIE	His nickname
WEIGHTLESS	An astronaut pet
WELBY	"Marcus Welby, M.D."
WELCH	For a Welsh corgi
WELCOME	For a rottweiler (ha, ha)
WELK	For a man whose name is Lawrence
WELLER	For a pet that looks for wells
WELLINGTON	For a pet that likes walking in the rain, or wears boots
WELTY	For a person allergic to their cat, or a Eudora fan
WEMBLEY	For a Brittany spaniel
WENDEL	For an English setter
WENDOVER	A Sussex spaniel
WENDY	A *Peter Pan* character

WENTWORTH	The first female pro golfer to win more than one million dollars
WERTMULLER	A pet for an aspiring female director
WESLEY	For a blue and white Scottish fold
WESTERN	For someone who doesn't like to ride eastern
WESTHEIMER	For a pet that knows everything there is to know about sex
WESTIE	For a western pet
WESTING-HOUSE	For a pet that can light up your life
WESTMORE-LAND	For a pet that likes to take command
WESTON	For a Glen of Imaal terrier . . . has a "cocky fighting Irish spirit"
WET BLANKET	For a pet that doesn't travel well
WHARTENBY	A long-haired Saint Bernard
WHARTON	For a family with aspirations for its child to go to business school
WHATEVER	For someone very laid-back. Also, perfect for the mixed breed
WHEATCAKE	Another for the wheaten terrier
WHEATLY	My friend's soft-coated wheaten terrier
WHEATON	It used to be a very popular university
WHEELER DEALER	A used car salesman's pet
WHEELIE	For a pet good on a bike
WHEEZIE	For a pet that sneezes a lot
WHIG	The party running against Martin Van Buren in 1836. They lost.
WHIMSY	My friend's miniature poodle
WHISKERS	My friend's husband

WHISKEY	Same as Brandy. Everyone is into liquor names.
WHISTLER	As long as it's a mother
WHISTLER'S MOTHER	For a pet that sits all day
WHITBREAD	For a white Manx
WHITE CASTLE	For a pet that will only eat square hamburgers
WHITE CHOCOLATE	For a black and white pet of any kind
WHITE FOOT	For a pet with a white foot
WHITE GOLD	For a pet that doesn't want to be flashy
WHITEHALL	For someone who likes British politics
WHITE HOUSE	For someone who likes American politics
WHITE RUSSIAN	For someone who likes Russian politics
WHITE SOCKS	For someone who likes baseball politics
WHITEY	For someone who drives a Ford
WHITMAN	For someone who likes to sample
WHITNEY	For someone from Houston
WHITTIER	A town in California where my first best friend moved to when I was four . . . Kathy
WHIZ KID	For a pet very easy to train
WHIZZER	Definitely for a male animal
WHODUNIT	For a mystery fan
WHO LOVESYA	For a Telly Savalas fan
WHOLESALE	A shopper's pet
WHOLESALER	A pet that sells to the trade only
WHOLE WHEAT	Another good name for a wheaten terrier

WHOOPIE	For a happy pet
WHOPPER	For a big pet
WHYLE	For a boxer
WICKED WITCH	For a pet that refuses to be house trained
WIDMARK	For a Richard fan
WIENER SCHNITZEL	For a dachshund
WIGGLES	For a worm
WIGWAM	A rounded dwelling made from woven mats or birchbark over poles
WILBUR	The pig in *Charlotte's Web*
WILCOX	For any of your English breeds
WILDBERRY	For a ruddy wild Abyssinian
WILD BILL	See Bill Hickock
WILDCAT	If you've got it, you'll know it.
WILDE	For someone who likes Oscar
WILDER	For someone who likes Gene or Laura Ingalls
WILDFIRE	For any animal that produces copiously and often
WILDFLOWER	For a blue silver patched tabby Maine Coon
WILD RICE	A cook's pet
WILD THING	It makes your heart sing
WILEY	For a very clever pet
WILHELM	For a German long-haired pointer
WILKIE	A failed presidential candidate. Pair with Stevenson
WILKINS	For an English mastiff
WILLARD	For a pet that can tell the weather

WILLFUL	For a pet that's hard to train
WILLIAM	For an heir to the throne
WILLIAMS	For the butler of the heir to the throne
WILLIE	I see this for a cat, don't you?
WILLIE WONKA	You know, the chocolate factory . . . perfect for a dark brown pet
WILLIS	Bruce!
WILLOW	For a blue-cream point Himalayan
WILLOWBREEZE	For a blue-cream point Himalayan that likes to go outdoors
WILLY	For a free pet
WILMA	Fred's wife in ''The Flintstones''
WILSHIRE	For a boulevard in Los Angeles, or a brown California spangled
WILSON	Dennis the Menace's neighbor
WILT	For a very tall pet
WILTON	How you feel standing next to that very tall pet
WIMBLEDON	For an avid tennis aficionado
WIMPY	For a meek pet
WINCHELL	Walter
WINCHESTER	A cathedral or a weapon, take your pick
WINDJAMMER	A sailor's pet
WINDSOR	For someone in the tie business
WINDY	For a pet with a lot of gas
WINFREY	For a devoted Oprah fan
WINGER	For a bird
WINGS	Also for a bird
WINIFRED	I love this. Just about any female would be gorgeous with this name.

WINK	For the cat that swallowed the canary
WINKLER	Very cute. As is Henry
WINNEDOO	For a blue mitted ragdoll
WINNIE	For a Pooh
WINONA	For someone who likes horses
WINSTON	How quickly we forget
WINTHROP	This is a wonderful male name. Just imagine having both Winifred and Winthrop (maybe it's too much).
WIPEOUT	A surfer's pet
WIPPLE	For someone into toilet paper
WIRETAP	A detective's pet
WISDOM	A dentist's pet
WISECRACK	A comedian's pet
WISE GUY	A mobster's pet
WISENHEIMER	For a pet that's too smart for its own good
WISTERIA	A gardener's pet
WITHERS	A bad gardener's pet
WITHHOLDER	For a very independent cat
WITNESS	For a pet that sleeps on your bed
WIZARD	A genius' pet
WOLFE	For a Yorkshire terrier
WOLFGANG	A German shepherd
WOLFMAN	A name for a Jack Russell terrier
WONDER	For a pet that's a little out of it
WONDER BREAD	For a white fluffy pet
WONG	For someone who's never right
WOODROW	For a Wilson fan
WOODSON	For a redtick coonhound

WOODSTOCK	Snoopy's bird
WOODWARD	A journalist's pet
WOODY	For a woodpecker
WOOFER	A basenji (doesn't bark)
WOOFSTOCK	For a basenji breeder
WOOLLY	For a sheep
WOOLWORTH	For a cheap sheep
WORDSWORTH	For a parrot
WORTH AVENUE	For someone who likes to be re-minded of the good life and Florida
WRANGLER	Good for a Jack Russell . . . or some-one who lives in jeans
WRECKER	Also good for a Jack Russell
WRINKLER	Chinese Shar-pei
WRINKLES	Chinese Shar-pei . . . again
WRITE-OFF	An accountant's pet
WUNDERKIND	For a parrot with an incredible vocabulary
WUZZIE	For a Devon rex . . . 'cause, he wasn't fuzzy, wuz he?
WYATT	For a person who longs to go west
WYATT EARP	For a pet that's quick on the draw
WYCLIFF	What you ask your dog Cliff after an accident
WYLER	For a Gordon setter
WYMAN	For a brown classic tortie American curl
WYNETTE	For a Tennessee treeing brindle
WYNTER	For a Siberian husky
WYOMING	For a horse

XANADU	For an animal that resembles Olivia Newton-John
XAVIER	For anyone into big bands, dancing, and swanky dinners
XENIA	Daughter in Moussorgsky's *Boris Godunov*
XENON	A colorless animal whose presence is barely felt
XENOPHON	Greek historian, disciple of Socrates
XEROX	Siamese twins, or copycats
XERXES	For Persians
XIA	Chow chows, Chinese crested dog, Shih Tzu
XL	Though an excellent example of its breed, it still can't spell
X MAN	Heroic with its own sense of reality
XMAS	Sled dogs with red noses
X-RATED	Manx or Japanese bobtail (tailless varieties)
X RAY	Black and white calicos, or animals caught in headlights
XYLOPHONE	A group of singing canaries. Individually identified by note

YAKOV	Borzois, Russian blues
YACHTSMAN	An expensive fish
YACKER	Parrots, macaws
YAEL	For a serious, studious pet
YAGI	Baby talk. Save it for small, slightly misbehaving pets.
YAGO	For a pet that likes sangria
YAKI TORI	For a pet that likes Japanese food (or birds you're planning to eat)
YALE	Makes you the show-off
YAM	Orange-colored animals
YANA	The iguana
YANCY	Derringer. Cowboy country
YANG	Any Asian breed ... chow chows, Shih Tzus, etcetera
YANGTZE	You have three Asian breeds (chow chows, Shih Tzus, etcetera), Yang A and Yang B
YANNI	For a songbird
YANKEE	American bred, particularly dogs that run after your cat till you have to stop and order them home

YANKEE DOODLE	Your pet resembles James Cagney
YAPHET	Pronounced *ya-feh* ... means "pretty" in Hebrew
YAQUI	Another one for parrots and macaws
YARBOROUGH	For experienced bridge players
YARDLEY	A clean, fresh smelling pet that lives outdoors
YARD MASTER	A successfully housebroken suburban pet
YARDSTICK	A dressmaker's pet ... also good for a dachshund
YARMULKE	Has a dark patch on top of its head
YARNIE	Tall, tailed pets
YARROW	Any yellow animal
YASAHIRO	For a Japanese bobtail, akita, or Japanese spaniel
YASMIN	For Persians
YASSER	For a pharaoh dog, or a real mutt
YASTRZEMSKI	Boston terriers. Nickname Yaz
YATES	You have a poetic streak, you just can't spell
YA TIDDLE	Thick necks
YAZ	*See* Yastrzemski
YEASTY	Chameleons and fish
YEATS	Poet
YELLER	It's to an old yellow Lab like Lassie is to a collie ... also good for a loud parrot
YELLOW BELL	Appropriate for a variety of birds. Also to spooked cats and neurotic dogs
YELLOWSTONE	Reptiles

YELTSIN	For a Siberian husky, Russian wolf-hound, Afghan, or borzoi
YEOMAN	Working English setters
YEOMAN OF THE GUARD	Dobermans, German shepherds, etcetera
YERTLE	The turtle
YES	For a basketball fan
YESTERDAY	Pet beetle
YEVTUSHENK	*See* Yeltsin ... any of the Russian breeds
YIDDISH	A particularly expressive parrot
YIN	The female half of a chow chow pair
YIPPIE	Coat looks tie-dyed
YITZHAK	Begins as a rebel, ends as a leader
YMCA	Any pet that knows how to move its arms to make the letters of the song
YO	A very cool pet
YODA	A pug would be perfect, or a bulldog
YODEL	A singing canary
YODELS	A chorus of singing canaries
YOGA	For a very quiet, agile pet
YOGI	For a very quiet, agile pet that looks good in white
YOGI BEAR	A large example of Yogi ... or its complete opposite
YOGURT	White vegetarian pets with no dairy allergies
YOKE	A bird, snake, or ox
YOKO	Japanese bobtails
YOLANDA	Parrots, macaws, talkative animals
YONA	For a lazy pet. It just sounds like a lazy name, sort of like "yawn"

YOO HOO	Chocolate Labs, chocolate point Siameses
YORBA	The great . . . though not as great as Zorba
YORK	Any Yorkshire terrier
YORKE	Not just any Yorkshire terrier
YORTY	Suggests a nickname for a longer version that's been in the family for five generations
YOSEMITE	Reptiles
YOUCON	For a toucan
YOUNG	For a pet that thinks its father knows best
YOUNGMAN	For a pet that thinks it's a comedian
YOYO	Pet frogs
YUBA	Snakes, frogs, lizards, and pigs
YUCATAN	Chihuahuas, Mexican hairless
YUCHI	For tiny, cute, affectionate lap sitters
YUKI	Though you love it, it does some disgusting things
YUKON	For Alaskan malamutes, Eskimo dogs
YUKON KING	From the fifties TV show . . . he was a husky
YUL	Anything hairless
YULE	A Christmas present
YUM YUM	A tramp
YUPPIE	A pet with a Rolex and a Land Rover
YURI	The Russian breeds again
YUSUF	Songbirds with a jazz repertoire
YVETTE	Sexy with heavy eyeliner markings
YVONNE	A more mature sexuality

ZABAGLIONE	Cream-colored pets ... something all whipped up, like a bichon frise
ZABAR	For a pet that lives in New York and likes good deli food
ZABRISKIE	Any pointer
ZACCHEUS	Biblical name
ZACH	A short pet, or a pet with a short attention span
ZACHARIAS	An Old Testament animal
ZACHARY	A twentieth-century animal
ZADIE	Means ''grandma'' in Yiddish
ZADORA	Sexy, pouty, passable voice
ZAFTIG	Any pet with an ample figure
ZAHIR	For any pet that likes heat
ZAKAIAH	Goes well with Jebediah and Obediah
ZALMAN	Fish
ZAMBONI	Huskys ... can't you just see them pulling a sled across the ice rink?
ZANE	Pet horse
ZANE GREY	Pet gray horse (but, all kidding aside, remember the ''Zane Grey Theater''?)

ZANG	Songbirds with German accents
ZANUCK	A pet into old movies
ZANY	For the pet that makes you laugh
ZANZA	Any particularly foreign and strong-looking pet
ZANZIBAR	Poicephalus parrots, African greg parrots, or any exotic-sounding pet
ZAPATA	A pet that every time you look at it you want to yell, "Viva Zapata!"
ZAPPA	Long, scraggly hair, funny, irreverent
ZAPPER	It fights with you for the control
ZAPPI	Attack dogs. The "i" is disarming and will catch attackers off guard
ZARA	For any of the female Russian breeds, though historically it's appropriate for dalmatians
ZASU	Pitts . . . Wouldn't this be good for a small pet?
ZAW	The macaw
ZAZEN	Meditation in zen Buddhism. Use it on a turtle to explain what goes on inside that shell.
ZAZI	Female French poodles
ZEALOT	A pet that guards its toys, food, children, and owner's children very well.
ZECH	Zecharia's nickname
ZECHARIA	A twist on Zacharias
ZEE ZEE	For your smaller breeds
ZEFF	You already used up Jeff, Heff, and Ref
ZEFFER	The full name
ZEFFIRELLI	Italian stage and screen director
ZEISS	Cats with extraordinary vision

ZEITGEIST   Any pet that's the current rage

ZELDA   You can go two ways. First, anything with a twitchy nose ("Dobie Gillis"), or second, F. Scott's match

ZELIG   Chameleons with glasses

ZELLA   Reminds you of a cheap wine

ZELLE   Female French poodles

ZEN   *See* Zazen

ZENITH   For a couch potato, or the top of its breed

ZENOBIA   Shelled pets ... turtles

ZEPH   Zephan's nickname

ZEPHAN   A Russian Stephen

ZEPHANIAH   For a Russian blue or borzoi

ZEPHYR   A bird from the West

ZEPHYRUS   A bird that acts like it's from the West

ZEPPELIN   A bird that's lost the ability to fly

ZERBE   A Greek pet

ZERLINA   Character in Mozart's *Don Giovanni*

ZERO   Dalmatians

ZESTA   For a happy-go-lucky pet that makes the most of life

ZESTY   Not exactly lusty, peppy, or zippy, sort of a combination

ZETTA   Not quite as active as Zesta and Zesty

ZEUS   An animal of the highest authority

ZEZE   To be said in a high voice

ZHOU EN-LAI   Any of the Asian breeds

ZHUKOV   A KGB sounding name ... Russian wolfhound, Samoyed, Karelian bear dog

ZIA	Makes me think of a Chia pet ... just water it and the hair keeps growing
ZIEGFELD	A pet that is either a folly or a great dancer
ZIFFI	A made-up name whose rhyme with iffy is not coincidental
ZIG ZAG	Tabbys, mice
ZIGGY	Of the cartoon fame
ZILCH	A pet you never wanted
ZILLION	Insect collection
ZIMBALIST	Stephanie for the nineties ... Efrem for the sixties, seventies, and eighties
ZIMMI	When you want the name to be a bit more exotic than Jimmy
ZINA	I believe that Zina Bethune played a nurse on the show "Nurses" in the sixties
ZINC	Blue point Balinese, blue point Birman, Cornish rex, silver Persian, etcetera
ZINCKY	Zinc's nickname
ZINDEL	For a spinster pet
ZINFANDEL	A wine lover's pet
ZING	Birds with irritating, high pitched voices
ZINGER	Hits its target every time
ZINNIA	Yet another flower to add to the list ... triple with Lily and Petunia
ZIP CODE	Homing pigeons, or a postman's pet
ZIPPER	A pet that knows how to keep quiet
ZIRCON	Fake but fairly convincing pedigree
ZIRCONIA	Same as above
ZITHER	Songbirds

ZITI	Snakes, dachshunds . . . tubular pets
ZIZI	A very endearing pet name
ZODIAC	Fish (or rams, bulls, crabs, lions, etcetera)
ZOE	Turkish Angoras
ZOISIA	A pet that loves to roll in the grass
ZOLA	French poodles
ZOLTAN	Powerful name. Good for a Great Dane or borzoi or anything big
ZOMBIE	Snake god of voodoo cults (yuck, I thought it was just someone who couldn't get it together)
ZONA	French word for shingles . . . save it for pets with shells
ZONK	For heavy sleepers
ZONTIA	For a very big feline
ZOOMER	Pet looking good in a helmet
ZOOM LENS	A photographer's pet
ZOOT SUIT	Brightly colored fish
ZORA	A female Zorro type
ZORBA	A pet with a lust for life (opposite of Zonk)
ZORI	Love means never having to say you're zori
ZORN	Sounds like a guard dog
ZOROASTER	Persians
ZORRO	My grandmother and I used to watch this together. Any pet that looks like it wears a mask.
ZOYA	For a Russian blue, Russian wolfhound, etcetera
ZSA ZSA	You own several sisters but have discarded all their mates

ZUBERRY
You're hoping that Ben and Jerry will name a flavor after it

ZUBIN
Give it a baton to go with its black tail

ZUBOV
A defensive pet that likes ice hockey

ZUCCHERO
A very popular Italian singer (pronounced "*zuckero*")

ZUCCHINI
A very popular vegetable ... good for snakes, iguanas, geckos

ZUCKER
For a sweet pet

ZUCKERMAN
For a pet that looks like it's a businessman

ZUCKIE
An even sweeter pet

ZUKOR
This sounds big, like a rottweiler

ZULA
The first Abyssinian cat to reach England

ZULU
Dobermans, German shepherds, rottweilers, etcetera

ZUNI
This is good for any of the hunting dogs

ZUPPA INGLESE
One of my very favorite desserts

ZURIEL
For a Russian blue

ZUTZKA
Good for a smaller breed, like a Cairn terrier, miniature poodle, Jack Russell terrier

ZUZI
For a Shih Tzu or Lhasa apso, a Persian or Egyptian mau

ZUZUSHI
For a very fast raw fish

ZWEIG
For a pet that can drink from a flask

ZWIEBACK   For a pet that can eat cookies from a box

ZWINDLER   For a pet that competes with your baby for the cookies

Doubles and Triples

For those of you lucky (or unlucky, as the case may be) to live with two or more pets, the following lists should give you some ideas for pairs (if you swallowed the argument that two can keep each other company while you're out) or trios (if the idea of three pets at once doesn't sound like chaos).

Of course, if you're one of those people who has a whole menagerie of pets at home then maybe these doubles and triples can point you toward something clever, but if you really want a quartet or quintet of names, you're on your own.

Doubles

ABBOTT & COSTELLO

ABERCROMBIE & FITCH

ADONIS & VENUS

ALICE & RALPH

ALVIN & AILEY

A.M. & F.M.

AMOS & ANDY

ANNETTE & FABIAN

ANNIE OAKLEY &
BUFFALO BILL

ANTONY & CLEOPATRA

ARAFAT &
GAZA STRIPPER

ARCHIE & BETTY

ARCHIE & EDITH

ARCHIE & JUGHEAD

ARI & JACKIE

ARSENIC & OLD LACE

ASTAIRE & ROGERS

AURORA & BOREALIS

BABBITT & MYRNA

BABE & RUTH

BACH & BEETHOVEN

BACON & EGGS

BAMBI & THUMPER

BARBIE & KEN

BARDOT & VADIM

BARNEY & BETTY

BARNEY & FRED

BARNUM & BAILEY

BATMAN & CATWOMAN

BATMAN & ROBIN

BEAVER & WALLY

BEEZUS & HENRY

BEEZUS & RAMONA

BEN & JERRY

BERT & ERNIE

BERT & NAN

BETAMAX & VHS

BEULAH & HAZEL

BILL & HILLARY

BLACK & WHITE

BLACKJACK & ROULETTE

BLONDIE & DAGWOOD

BLUE & CHIP

BOBBY DARIN & SANDRA DEE

BOGIE & BACALL

BOLOGNESE & MILANESE

BOLSHOI & MISHA

BONNIE & CLYDE

BORDEAUX & BEAUJOLAIS

BORIS & BELA

BORIS & KARLOFF

BORIS & NATASHA

BOSLEY & BRI

BOURGUIGNONNE & BERNAISE

BOW & ARROW

BRANDO & BOGART

BRI & BLUE

BRIDE & GROOM

BRIDGET & BERNIE

BRIGITTE & BARDOT

BRIOCHE & BAGUETTE

BRISTOL & CREAM

BROADWAY & TIMES SQUARE

BROOKS & BANCROFT

BRUCE & DEMI

BRYANT & KATIE

BUCKWHEAT & ALFALFA

BUNSEN & BEAKER

BURNS & ALLEN

BUSTER & BROWN

CAESAR & CLEOPATRA

CAGNEY & LACEY

CAGNEY & YANKEE DOODLE

CAIN & ABEL

CANDIDE & VOLTAIRE

CAPTAIN & TENNILLE

CARLO & SOPHIA

CAROL & CLARK

CARROT CAKE & BANANA BREAD

CARSON & LETTERMAN

CASSIUS CLAY & MUHAMMAD ALI

CATWOMAN & BRUCE

CHA-CHA & RUMBA

CHAMPAGNE & CAVIAR

CHANEL & ARPÉGE

CHARLES & CAMILLA	DA VINCI & LEONARDO
CHARLES & DIANA	DAY & NIGHT
CHARLEY & STEINBECK	DEMOCRAT & REPUBLICAN
CHARLIE CHAN & NUMBER ONE SON	DENIRO & STREEP
CHEWBACCA & C3PO	DENNIS & MR. WILSON
CHINA & PROCELAIN	DEVITO & SCHWARZENEGGER
CHIP & DALE	DIANA & FERGIE
CHURCHILL & THATCHER	DIANE & CARLA
CINDERELLA & PRINCE CHARMING	DIANE & FRASIER
CLARABELL & CHIEF THUNDERTHUD	DIANE & SAM
	DICK & JANE
CLARABELL & HOWDY DOODY	DICK & TRACY
CLARK & LOIS	DICKENS & COPPERFIELD
COCO & CHANEL	DIJON & HONEY
COKE & PEPSI	DISCO & ROCK AND ROLL
COLUMBUS & ISABELLA	DJ & CD
COPA & CABANA	DON QUIXOTE & DULCINEA
COWBOY & INDIAN	
CRACKER & JACK	DONALD & GOOFY
CRIMSON & CLOVER	DONNA & ALEX
CROCKETT & TUBBS	DONNA & RICHIE
CYRANO & ROXANNE	DOROTHY & OZ
DARRYL & STRAWBERRY	DORSEY & MILLER
DAVID & GOLIATH	DOW & JONES

DUKE & DUCHESS

DUKE ELLINGTON & COUNT BASIE

DWIGHT & MAMIE

EBONY & IVORY

ED & JOHNNY

ED & RALPH

ED & TRIXIE

EISENHOWER & NIXON

EITHER & OR

ELIOT & NESS

ELIZA DOOLITTLE & HENRY HIGGINS

ELOISE & PLAZA

ELVIS & PRISCILLA

FARRAH & RYAN

FAY & BETTINA

FERDINAND & ISABELLA

FERGIE & ANDREW

FESTER & LURCH

FETA & MOZZARELLA

FETTUCCINE & ALFREDO

FIBBER MCGEE & MOLLY

FILO & FAX

FLASH GORDON & BUCK ROGERS

FRANK & KATHIE LEE

FRANKIE & JOHNNY

FRANKLIN & ELEANOR

FRASIER & LILITH

FRED & ETHEL

FRED & GINGER

FREDDIE & FLOSSIE

FREEBIE & BEAN

FRICK & FRACK

F. SCOTT & FITZGERALD

FUNICELLO & AVALON

FUNK & WAGNALL

GABBY HAYES & NELLY BELLY

GABLE & LOMBARD

GARBO & DIETRICH

GARFIELD & ODIE

GENE AUTRY & GABBY HAYES

GEORGE & BARBARA

GEORGE & GRACIE

GEORGE & IRA

GIDGET & MOONDOGGIE

GILLIGAN & SKIPPER

GIMBEL'S & MACY'S

GIN & TONIC

GINGER & MARY ANN

GODFREY & IRENE

GOLDFINGER & BOND

GOLDIE & KURT

GOMEZ & MORTICIA

GOOBER & RAISINETTE

GORBIE & BRESCHNEV

GRANT & LEE

GREEN EGGS & HAM

GRIFFIN & SABINE

GUCCI & FENDI

GULLIVER & YAHOO

GUNS 'N' ROSES

GUY & GAL

HAIKU & POETRY

HAMLET & LAERTES

HAMLET & MACBETH

HAMLET & OPHELIA

HAM ON & RYE

HANS BRINKER & GRETEL

HANSEL & GRETEL

HARRY & LEONA

HARRY & WINSTON

HARVARD & RADCLIFFE

HARVARD & YALE

HAWKEYE & B. J.

HAWKEYE & PIERCE

HAWN & RUSSELL

HENNY & YOUNGMAN

HENRY & RIBSY

HERO & LEANDER

HIAWATHA & LONGFELLOW

HIM & HER

HODGE & PODGE

HOLLY GOLIGHTLY & CAT

HOLMES & WATSON

HOOK & PAN

HOPE & ANCHOR

HOSS & LITTLE JOE

HOT FUDGE & CHOCOLATE

HOT LIPS & FRANK

HOWARD & ROBIN

HOWDY DOODY & UNCLE BOB

HUGS & KISSES

HUMPHREY & BETTE

HUNKY & DORY

HUNTLEY & BRINKLEY

HURLY & BURLY

ICE CREAM & SPRINKLES

ICHABOD & CRANE

IKE & MAMIE

ILIAD & ODYSSEY

IPSO & FACTO

IRMALA & DUCE

ISH & KABIBBLE

ISHMAEL & MOBY DICK

JACK BENNY & ROCHESTER

JACOBY & MEYERS

JAKE & ELLWOOD

JANE EYRE & MR. ROCHESTER

JAMES BOND & MONEYPENNY

JAMES BROWN & STEVIE WONDER

JAN & DEAN

JEAN & JOHNNY

JEEVES & BERTIE

JEKYLL & HYDE

JIM & MARGARET

JIM & TAMMY

JIMMY & MR. WHITE

JOAN & DAVID

JOANIE & CHACHI

JOE & FRANK

JOE FRIDAY & BILL GANNON

JOHN & YOKO

JORDAN & MARSH

J.R. & BOBBY

JUNE & WARD

KARLOFF & LUGOSI

KATHARINE & SPENCER

KEN & BARBIE

KERMIT & MISS PIGGY

KGB (KAYGEE) & CIA (SEE-EYE)

KING & QUEEN

KING ARTHUR & GUINEVERE

KING ARTHUR & MERLIN

KING ARTHUR & SIR LANCELOT

KING LEAR & OTHELLO

KIPLING & KIM

KLINGER & RADAR

KLINK & SCHULTZ

KRAMDEN & NORTON

LADY & TRAMP

LADY CHATTERLEY & OLIVER

LADY GODIVA & FANNIE FARMER

LANCELOT & GUINEVERE

LAPIS & LAZULI

LAVERNE & SHIRLEY

LENNY & SQUIGGY

LENO & LETTERMAN

LERNER & LOWE

LEWIS & CLARK

L'IL ABNER & DAISY MAE

LINCOLN & MERCURY

LINUS & LUCY

LITTLE JOE & PA

LIZ & RICHARD

LIZ & RICHARD

LIZ & RICHARD

LIZ & RICHARD

LOIS & JIMMY

LONE RANGER & TONTO

LUCY & DESI

LUCY & ETHEL

LUCY & RICKY

LUGOSI & DRACULA

LUKE & LAURA

LUKE & PRINCESS LEIA

LYNDON & LADY BIRD

LYSANDER & HERMIA

MACDUFF & FIFE

MACKINTOSH & T.J.

MAGOO & BACKUS

MAJOR & MINOR

MARCEL & MARCEAU

MARCELLO & SOPHIA

MARCELLUS & HORATIO

MARSHAL DILLON & MISS KITTY

MAX & WILD THING

MAXWELL SMART & AGENT 99

MCGARRETT & DANO

MCGILLICUDY & RICARDO

MEAT & POTATOES

MELVIN & HOWARD

MERCEDES & PORSCHE

MERTZ & RICARDO

MICKEY & MINNIE

MIKADO & POOH-BAH

MILDRED & ELSIE

MILLY & OLLY

MILO & OTIS

MISS MARPLE & POIROT

MISS VICKY & TINY TIM

MOE & LARRY

MONTAGUE & CAPULET

MORK & MINDY

MOZART &
TCHAIKOVSKY

MRS. ROBINSON &
THE GRADUATE

MUHAMMAD ALI &
CASSIUS CLAY

MUTT & JEFF

MY MAN & GODFREY

NAPOLEON & JOSEPHINE

NATE & AL

NEIMAN & MARCUS

NICK & NORA

NORM & CARLA

NORTON & KRAMDEN

NORTON & TRIXIE

OEDIPUSS & ODEIPUP

O'HARA & BUTLER

ONYX & CORAL

OPRAH & PHIL

OSCAR & EMMY

OSCAR & FELIX

OXFORD & CAMBRIDGE

OZZIE & HARRIET

PABLO & PALOMA

PARSLEY & SAGE

PAT & VANNA

PEACHES & CREAM

PEANUT BUTTER & JELLY

PEBBLES & BAMM BAMM

PEE WEE REESE &
JACKIE ROBINSON

PENGUIN & JOKER

PERRY & DELLA

PETE & REPETE

PETER & CAPTAIN HOOK

PETER & TINKER BELL

PHIL & MARLO

PHILIP & ELIZABETH

PHYLLIS & FANG

PINKIE & LEE

PINOCCHIO & WOODY

PIROUETTE & MINUET

PITTER & PATTER

PLAIN & FANCY

POPEYE & OLIVE OYL

PORGY & BESS

PORSCHE & MERCEDES

PORTNOY & COMPLAINT

POT & PAN

PREAKNESS & BELMONT

PREPPIE & HIPPIE

PRINCE & PRINCESS

PRINCE CHARMING &
CINDERELLA

PULITZER & NOBEL

PUNCH & JUDY

PUSS & BOOTS

PYRAMUS & THISBE

QUEEN ANNE &
KING GEORGE

RALPH & ALICE

RAVEL & BOLERO

REGIS & KATHIE LEE

RHETT & SCARLETT

RHODA & PHYLLIS

RHYTHM & BLUES

RICK & CASABLANCA

RIDDLER & JOKER

RITZ & CARLTON

RITZ & CRACKER

ROB & LAURA

ROBIN HOOD &
MAID MARIAN

ROCK & DORIS

ROCK & ROLL

ROCKY & ADRIAN

ROCKY & BULLWINKLE

RODGERS &
HAMMERSTEIN

RODGERS & HART

ROMEO & JULIET

ROMULUS & REMUS

RONNIE & NANCY

ROONEY & HARDY

ROSALIND & JIMMY

ROSEMARY & BABY

ROSEMARY & THYME

ROUGH & READY

ROY ROGERS &
DALE EVANS

ROY ROGERS &
GABBY HAYES

ROY ROGERS &
GENE AUTRY

RUBY & SAPPHIRE

RUDOLPH & SANTA

RUM & COKE

SALINGER &
HEMINGWAY

SALLY & BUDDY

SALT 'N' PEPA

SALT & PEPPER

SALVADOR & DALÍ

SAMSON & DELILAH

SARGENT SCHULTZ &
COLONEL HOGAN

SCHULTZY & BOB

SCOTCH & SODA

SCOTT & ZELDA

SHAKESPEARE & TENNYSON

SHARI & LAMBCHOP

SHERIFF & DEPUTY

SHERIFF & MISS KITTY

SHERLOCK & HEMLOCK

SIEGFRIED & ROY

SILVER & TRIGGER

SIMON & GARFUNKEL

SKY KING & PENNY

SMITH & WESSON

SNOOPY & LINUS

SNOOPY & WOODSTOCK

SOCRATES & XANTHIPPE

SOPHIA & CARLO

SOUFFLÉ & MOUSSE

SPENSER & HAWK

SPENSER & SUSAN

SPIN & MARTY

SPOCK & KIRK

STAR & TREKKER

STARSKY & HUTCH

STING & AXL

STOCKS & BONDS

STOLI & ABSOLUT

SUGAR & SPICE

SULLIVAN & CROMWELL

SWASH & BUCKLE

SWEET & LOW

TAFT & HARTLEY

TEMPEST & TEAPOT

THE DONALD & MARLA

THELMA & LOUISE

THICK & THIN

THUNDER & LIGHTNING

THURSTON HOWELL III & LOVEY

TIFFANY & CARTIER

TIGER & LILY

TIME & NEWSWEEK

TIMEX & BULOVA

TIN MAN & COWARDLY LION

TIPPECANOE & TYLER

TOAST & JELLY

TOLKIEN & HOBBIT

TOLSTOY & KARENINA

TOM & JERRY

TONTO & LONE RANGER

TOODY & MULDOON

TRACK & FIELD

TRACY & HEPBURN

TRINIDAD & TOBAGO

TRISTAN & ISOLDE

TRIXIE & ALICE

TROILUS & CRESSIDA

T.S. & ELIOT

TUNNEY & DEMPSEY

TWEETY & SYLVESTER

UNCLE TONOOSE & DANNY

VALENTINE & PROTEUS

VAUGHN & KURIAKIAN

VENUS & EARTHA

VICTOR & VICTORIA

VIM & VIGOR

VINAIGRETTE & ROQUEFORT

VIOLET & DAISY

VIVALDI & RACHMANINOFF

VOLCKER & GREENSPAN

WAIT & ANDSEE

WENDY & NANA

WILKIE & STEVENSON

WILLARD & MR. G.

WINFREY & DONAHUE

WINWOOD & HIGH LIFE

WOLF & RED RIDING HOOD

YANKEE & DOODLE

ZEUS & APOLLO

ZSA ZSA & EVA

Triples

ABC • NBC • CBS

AGASSI • BORG • STICH

A. J. FOYT • UNSER • ANDRETTI

ALFRED • BATMAN • ROBIN

ALTO • SOPRANO • TENOR

AMOS • ANDY • KINGFISH

ARCHIE • BETTY • VERONICA

ARCHIE • BETTY • JUGHEAD

ARCHIE • EDITH • MEATHEAD

ASHE • LAVER • ROSEWALL

ASTRO • PADRE • RED

BACH • BEETHOVEN • RAVEL

BATMAN • ROBIN • ALFRED

BATMAN • CATWOMAN • VICKIE

BEAVER • WALLY • EDDIE

BEEZUS • RAMONA • HENRY

BELL • BOOK • CANDLE

BERT • ERNIE • BIG BIRD

BETTY • KATHY • BUD

BETTY • BARNEY • BAMM BAMM

BILLY • ALLISON • JANE

BOOGIE • LINDY • SWING

BORIS • NATASHA • BADENOV

BRANDON • DYLAN • STEVE

BRANDY • WHISKEY • SHOTSIE

BREWER • WHITE SOCK • RANGER

BRIOCHE • BAGUETTE • CROISSANT

BRYANT • KATIE • WILLARD

BUDDY • ROB • SALLY

BULLWINKLE • ROCKY • DUDLEY DO-RIGHT

CHA-CHA • MAMBO • RUMBA

CHANEL • ARPÈGE • BRUTE

CHANEL • BORGHESE • LANCÔME

CHARLES • DI • CAMILLA

CHIFFON • ORGANDY • ORGANZA

CINDERELLA • PRINCE CHARMING • SLIPPER

CLARABELL • HOWDY DOODY • BUFFALO BOB

COBB • BABE • GEHRIG

COCO • CHANEL • PARIS

COLETTE • YVETTE • SUZETTE

COLONEL KLINK • LEBEAU • SCHULTZ

COSBY • STILLS • NASH

D'ARTAGNAN • ARAMIS • PORTHOS

DEMOCRAT • REPUBLICAN • INDEPENDENT

DIANE • SAM • FRASIER

DICK • JANE • SPOT

DIMAGGIO • MILLER • MONROE

DOBIE • ZELDA • GILLIS

DONALD • HOT LIPS • FRANK

DON DIEGO • ZORRO • MASK

DONNA • KELLY • BRENDA

DOROTHY • BLANCHE • ROSE

007 • GOLDFINGER • OCTAPUSSY

DUCHESS • DUKE • COUNT

EAT • DRINK • BEMERRY

FENDI • GUCCI • MARK CROSS

FERGIE • ANDREW • ELIZABETH

FETA • MOZZARELLA • BRIE

FRAZIER • FOREMAN • ALI

FRED • ETHEL • LUCY

FRIAR TUCK • MAID MARIAN • ROBIN HOOD

F. SCOTT • ZELDA • FITZGERALD

GENE AUTRY • ROY ROGERS • SLIM PICKENS

GEORGE • GRACIE • HARRY VON ZELL

GIANT • DODGER • BRAVE

GRAF • SELES • SABATINI

GRIFFITH • JOYNER • JACKIE

GROUCHO • HARPO • ZEPPO

GUGGENHEIM • METROPOLITAN • FRICK

GYPSY • ROSE • LEE

HAMBURGER • HOTDOG • FRIES

HAMLET • OHPELIA • MACBETH

HARPO • GROUCHO • CHICO

HARVARD • YALE • PRINCETON

HAWKEYE • HOT LIPS • FRANK

HAWKEYE • PIERCE • POTTER

HEART • DIAMOND • SPADE

HOGAN • LEBEAU • SCHULTZ

HOT FUDGE • CHOCOLATE • SPRINKLES

HOT LIPS • FRANK • KLINGER

HOWARD STERN • ROBIN • STUTTERING JOHN

HOWDY DOODY • UNCLE BOB • CLARABELL

IMELDA • MANILA • PUMPS

INKSTER • COCKERILL • MCGILL

JACK • BENNY • ROCHESTER

JANE • WORKOUT • TED

JIM • MAGARET • BETTY

JIMMY • LOIS • CLARK

JOAN • JACKIE • COLLINS

JOHN • PHILIP • SOUSA

JOHN • PAUL • GEORGE

JOYNER • KOCH • IVAN

JUNE • WARD • BEAVER

KENTUCKY DERBY • PREAKNESS • BELMONT

KERMIT • MISS PIGGY • OSCAR

KING • QUEEN • JACK

KING • PRINCE • PRINCESS

KING • QUEEN • DUKE

KING • COURT • GOOLAGONG

KING ARTHUR • GUINEVERE • LANCELOT

KLINGER • RADAR • B.J.

KOOKLA • FRAN • OLLIE

LARRY • DARRYL • DARRYL

LAVERNE • SHIRLEY • SQUIGGY

LISTON • TYSON • HOLYFIELD

LITTLE JOE • PA • HOSS

LOIS • JIMMY • PERRY

LONE RANGER • TONTO • SILVER

LUCY • PEANUTS • LINUS

LUCY • SKY • DIAMONDS

LUCY • RICKY • FRED

MANNY • MOE • JACK

MANTLE • MAYS • RUTH

MARIGOLD • PETUNIA • PUSSY WILLOW

MARY • PHYLLIS • RHODA

MASON • STREET • DRAKE

MAYBELLINE • CLINIQUE • REVLON

MCENROE • CONNORS • VILAS

MEDITERRANEAN • PACIFIC • ATLANTIC

MICKEY • MINNIE • DONALD DUCK

MISS LANE • MR. KENT • MR. WHITE

MISS MARPLE • MRS. FLETCHER • POIROT

MOE • LARRY • CURLY

MONEY MARKET • MUTUAL FUND • CD

MORTICIA • GOMEZ • FESTER

MR. WHITE • KENT • MISS LANE

MURPHY • CORKY • FRANK

NAVRATILOVA • EVERT • AUSTIN

NEWS • WEATHER • TRAFFIC

NICK • NORA • ASTA

NICKLAUS • PLAYER • TREVINO

NIÑA • PINTA • SANTA MARIA

NIXON • BUSH • FORD

NORM • VERA • CARLA

ORANTES • NEWCOMBE • NASTASE

ORIOLE • RED SOCK • INDIAN

OZZIE • HARRIET • RICKY

PABLO • PALOMA • PICASSO

PANSY • ROSE • VIOLET

PAUL • RINGO • GEORGE

PEANUTS • POPCORN • CRACKER JACK

PEBBLES • WILMA • FRED

PENGUIN • JOKER • ROBIN

PENNE • MACARONI • RAVIOLI

PERRY • DELLA • PAUL

PETER • NANA • CAPTAIN HOOK

PETER PAN • TINKER BELL • WENDY

PETUNIA • GARDENIA • GLADIOLA

PICASSO • MATISSE • KANDINSKY

PIERCE • B.J. • POTTER

PIERRE • PLAZA • REGENCY

PLAZA • PENINSULA • ST. REGIS

POPEYE • OLIVE OYL • SWEET PEA

PORSCHE • MERCEDES • VOLKSWAGEN

PRINCE • HEAD • WILSON

PRIVATE • LIEUTENANT • COLONEL

QUESTION • PERIOD • EXCLAMATION

RALPH • LAUREN • POLO

REEBOK • FILA • NIKE

RICK • ILSA • CASABLANCA

RINGO • STARR • DRUMMER

ROLEX • TIMEX • BULOVA

ROY • DALE • TRIGGER

SAMPRAS • EDBERG • BECKER

SCARLETT • RHETT • ASHLEY

SECRETARIAT • BOLD FORBES • SEATTLE SLEW

SHAKESPEARE • MACBETH • PORTIA

SHERLOCK • DR. WATSON • HOLMES

SMALL • MEDIUM • LARGE

SNAP • CRACKLE • POP

SNOOPY • WOODSTOCK • LUCY

SONNY • CROCKETT • TUBBS

SONY • PANASONIC • SHARP

SOUP • SANDWICH • DESSERT

SPAULDING • PENN • WILSON

SPENSER • HAWK • SUSAN

SPINKS • HOLMES • NORTON

STALLONE • ROCKY • RAMBO

STENGEL • HODGES • WEAVER

STOCKS • BONDS • TREASURIES

SUMMER • SPRING • AUTUMN

SUPERMAN • BATMAN • SPIDERMAN

SWEET • LOW • SUGAR

TIFFANY • CARTIER • BULGARI

TIN MAN • COWARDLY LION • WIZARD

TOM • DICK • HARRY

TUNNEY • DEMPSEY • SHARKEY

UNCLE TONOOSE • DANNY • RUSTY

VENUS • MARS • JUPITER

VIOLET • DAISY • LILY

WASHINGTON • LINCOLN • ROOSEVELT

WHOLE WHEAT (WHEATLY) • RYE • PUMPERNICKEL

WOODSTOCK • LINUS • LUCY

YANKEES • DODGERS • METS

ZINNIA • LILY • PETUNIA